Scoping the Social

Scoping the Social

An introduction to the practice of social theory

Anthony Woodiwiss

Open University Press

Open University Press
McGraw-Hill Education
McGraw-Hill House
Shoppenhangers Road
Maidenhead, Berkshire
England SL6 2QL

email: enquiries@openup.co.uk
world wide web: www.openup.co.uk

and Two Penn Plaza, New York, NY 1012–2289
USA

First published 2005

A catalogue record of this book is available from the British Library

ISBN-10: 0 335 21676 5 (pb)   0 335 21677 3 (hb)
ISBN-13: 9 780 335 216 765 (pb)   9 780 335 216 772 (hb)

Library of Congress Cataloging-in-Publication Data
CIP data has been applied for

Typeset by BookEns Ltd, Royston, Herts.
Printed and bound in Poland by OZGraf S.A.
www.polskabook.pl

For Frank Pearce

If I have had any good ideas
they are most likely to have arisen
as a consequence of conversations
with my dear friend Frank.

He had always, up to now, worked successfully under the aegis of
a great system (Marx, Sartre, Brecht, Semiology, the Text). Today,
it seems to him that he writes more openly, more unprotectedly;
nothing sustains him, unless there are still patches of bypassed
languages (for in order to speak one must seek support from other
texts). He says this without the infatuation which may
accompany all declarations of independence, and without the pose
of melancholy adopted to avow solitude; but rather in order to
account to himself for the feeling of insecurity which possesses
him today and, still more perhaps, the vague torment of a
recession toward the minor thing, the old thing he is when 'left to
himself'.

Roland Barthes, *Roland Barthes*

Contents

List of figures

Introduction
Practising social theory

Theory ... *noun* ... *a system of ideas or statements explaining something, from Greek* theoria *contemplation, speculation, sight, from* theoros *spectator, [which is] from the base of* theasthai *to look on* ...

(Shorter Oxford Dictionary)

Scope ... *verb,* American informal *to look at something or someone to see what they are like*

(Chambers Dictionary of Contemporary English)

Why learn how to theorize? The short answer is 'because social theory represents the core of a family of disciplines, most importantly sociology and such interdisciplinary areas as cultural studies, human geography, criminology, and media studies.' Typically, social theory textbooks are *about* theories and what other professionals have made of them and they are often very good in these terms. However, what they should also be about but are not, at least in any direct way, is how to use, criticize or contribute to the development of theory.[1] In my view, this missing dimension reflects the fact that the typical textbook tends to describe and discuss theories as finished items rather than as transitory crystallizations of practical reasoning in a research context. In stressing that theory should not be regarded as a self-contained topic but rather as an aspect of the larger, always ongoing, enterprise that is social research, my position differs markedly from that developed so inventively in recent years by Anthony Giddens: 'Social theory has the task of providing conceptions of the nature of human social activity and of the human agent which can be *placed in the service* of empirical work' (Giddens 1984: xvii, emphasis added). For me, and for a reason that will shortly be provided, it is pointless and sometimes even intellectually dangerous to engage in creative theoretical work (as distinct from commentary on such work) without or even before engaging in or with pertinent empirical research. Accordingly, throughout what follows and in order to make the particularity of my position clear, I will use the terms 'practitioner' or 'social scientist' as positive alternatives to 'theorist' wherever this is justified and stylistically possible.

1

One result of the currently prevailing approach to writing about social theory is that students often have considerable difficulty relating what they learn about theory to their other courses, projects, dissertations and even doctoral theses, let alone producing theory for themselves. The present text has been designed to address this difficulty in a way that will be helpful in different ways to a wide range of readers. The approach to social theory adopted here is derived from my books *Social Theory After Postmodernism* (Woodiwiss 1990a) and *The Visual in Social Theory* (Woodiwiss 2001) and it involves recovering the ancient Greek sense of theory as a form of visual work. Thus the reason why I consider it pointless to engage in theorizing without simultaneously engaging in or with pertinent empirical research is because one cannot look without looking at something. If you try the danger is that you will end up thinking not only that what is in your mind is what you are seeing but also that only your own mind can be known. The latter position is what the ancient Greeks called solipsism, and in my view it is the besetting sin of much contemporary social theory, as is signified, almost literally, by the widespread preoccupation with the issue of identity.

For me, and in the most general terms, social theory consists of abstract statements about the external social world produced in the light of substantive research and for the purpose of doing visual work. That is, theorizing is not the product of simply looking at the world but of purposely constructed modes of looking with the result that it is part and parcel of a larger process that involves and allows: *summarizing* data so that others may see what you have seen; *analysing and explaining* what you have seen; and, in general, the *envisioning* or *re-envisioning* of the social and so preparing it for further study. As a consequence, Part 1 – The Theory of Social Life – begins with a justification for the view that theorizing represents a variety of visual work before going on to describe in successive, brief chapters the different ways in which the abstract statements that do such work may be produced, as prescribed by the rationalist, empiricist, realist, and interpretivist/social-constructionist traditions. The final chapter of Part 1 is intended to provide some insights into what goes on within the different kinds of sites of theoretical practice (the study, the reading group, the research centre, the knowledge corporation, and the 'field'). This is in order that you may begin both to appreciate the practical interconnections between philosophical assumptions, theories and methods, and to imagine yourself engaging in different modes of theoretical work. In general terms, Part 1 provides information that should allow you to orient yourself in relation to most of the varieties of theory you are likely to come across. More particularly, it provides a series of templates as to how you might go about producing theory, templates that can be compared, contrasted, combined, copied, and of course refined or indeed rejected. Part 1 will feature the usual suspects (Karl Marx, Max Weber, and Emile Durkheim), plus Peter Winch and the generally excluded American empiricist tradition. It will, however, be less concerned with the details of their concepts and the relations between these concepts, which are well-described in the existing textbooks, and much more concerned with *how* they theorized; that is, with providing simple, schematic, usable, and indeed visual descriptions/evocations of their assumptions as to the nature of theoretical picturing and the consequences these assumptions have for both their substantive concepts and their articulations of these concepts as theories. In short, theory will be presented as an integral part of an ongoing research process that has philosophical, methodological, and empirical as well as conceptual aspects.

Part 2 – The Social Life of Theory – outlines some major postclassical instances and lines of theoretical work in the course of a schematic demonstration of what is involved in making a particular kind of radical theoretical intervention. It opens by explaining why I am unhappy with the current consequences of what has been called the 'linguistic' or, my preference, 'inward' turn among social and cultural researchers with its resulting methodological stress on reflexivity or the gaining of an appreciation of the constitutive role of personal assumptions, commitments and biases in the production of theory. The chapter then goes on to look at the way in which an understanding of the relationship between power and knowledge may be derived from the work of Marx, Georg Lukacs, Antonio Gramsci, Ferdinand de Saussure, and Michel Foucault. The reason for providing such an understanding is that it should enable you to begin to get to grips with one of the principal problems faced by all who produce or use theory. This is the problem created by the fact that, contrary to the beliefs of the advocates of the current mode of reflexivity, but like any other cultural artefact, theory has a life of its own that is rooted in wider intellectual and social con-ditions, many of which cannot be controlled by individuals or even whole academic disciplines. One consequence of theory having a life of its own is that theoretical practice is fraught with intellectual danger, especially in the case of the theoretical commentator whose thinking is not disciplined by the necessity of grappling with undeniably present external objects, which are therefore resistant to the totally free expression of the theoretical will. In the absence of such discipline it can be very difficult to escape extra-sociological influences, whether borne by the winds of politics, fashion or whatever, with the result that one's work may become, at one extreme, ideological or, at the other, simply and self-indulgently palimpsestic (writing upon writing). It is therefore important, not only that practitioners are creative but also that, like poker or *mah jong* players, they possess the capacities both to be self-critical and to hold their nerve in the sense of exhibiting a certain, possibly foolhardy, intellectual courage.

The remainder of the second part develops the idea of theory having a life of its own and outlines an approach to the practice of reflexivity, inspired by the work of Foucault and Pierre Bourdieu, that is very different to the presently prevailing one. This alternative approach is then used to provide a critical account of some of the key developments in social theory after two significant changes in its environment: first, the integration of the United States, with its distinctive social concerns as well as theoretical and methodological traditions, into the sociological universe; and second, the arrival of globalization and, with it, Asia in the sociological consciousness. These accounts apply the analytical tools and strategies associated with what I term 'ordinary realism' (see below, pp. 32–3) to: first, explain the success of what have commonly come to be regarded as 'winner' concepts (modernity, culture, agency, identity, discourse, and reflexivity) and theories (feminism, postmodernism, structuration theory, and neo-institutionalism); and second, suggest that the supposed 'loser' concepts (capitalism, social structure, ideology, class, and status) may be making a comeback in the reinvented form of what I call *neoclassical social theory* (Woodiwiss 2001: 13–14).

Apart from providing a way of presenting some familiar material in a provocative and, I hope, therefore stimulating manner, there are three main reasons for undertaking such a demonstration. First, to show that understanding theory as comprising a socially conditioned repertoire of modes of visualization can enhance one's capacity for creative as well as critical theoretical work. Second, to show that it is important to be aware and respectful of wider intellectual and social developments, including those on the margins, where it is otherwise commonly assumed that only intellectual dinosaurs and mountebanks may be found and/or that social life is barbaric. I remember coming across a copy of Frederick von Hayek's book *The Road To Serfdom* (1944) as an undergraduate and laughing out loud at what seemed to me to be its desperately old-fashioned critique of socialism and the welfare state – little did I know that Margaret Thatcher would later form a very different opinion of the thinker whose thought made it possible for her to become an ism. Currently, I feel that sociologists are likely to be similarly wrongfooted in the future because they still consider China and Asia more generally to be subject to a process of inevitable and necessary Westernization rather than the probable source of distinctive global social forces capable of initiating changes in the way in which life is lived in the West. Third, inspired by Ian Craib's (1998) pathbreaking essay on the 'psychodynamics of theory', I wish to show or warn that theoretical work can be psychologically demanding and even rough, as I have already implied by my earlier use of the harsh American vernacular terminology of 'winners' and 'losers'. Some people have a great deal of difficulty separating themselves from their theoretical work with the result that considerable amounts of emotional energy may sometimes be invested in either the defence of their own theoretical position or the critique of the positions held by others with the result, for example, that certain friendships may be impossible or put at risk, and all this despite the fact that little or nothing can be guaranteed by way of a return on this investment in terms of improved understanding. Finding a balance between the emotional commitment necessary for creative work and the self-amused, ironic detachment necessary to ride out the disappointments that almost inevitably follow can be very difficult. Chapters 7 and 8 look at 'winner' theory; that is, at the conceptual and methodological consequences of the United States' rise to sociological prominence. Chapter 9 looks at 'loser' theory and outlines both its largely unnoticed but continuing development in the form of neoclassical theory, and the significance of globalization (and more particularly Asia's re-entry into the sociological universe) for creating the possibility of reviving interest in such theory and its signature concept – social structure.

Although what follows may be read on its own, it would be best to read it alongside not only more conventional theory and methods textbooks (which commonly provide much more detailed accounts of the theories and research strategies to be discussed here) but also alongside primary sources. I wish to stress the importance of reading the latter because it is only when you can read and understand the primary texts themselves that you may regard yourself as theoretically literate, let alone as able to use the ideas contained in such texts. Making use of primary texts is not as difficult as might be imagined, however, since the primary practitioners frequently explain their work far more clearly than any commentator. I have therefore included, but only explained where absolutely necessary, a large number of rather long extracts from primary sources in order to help you attain the confidence to read such texts for yourself – that is, I have purposely made it virtually impossible for you to follow the argument without reading the extracts.

Finally, two 'health warnings' are necessary. The first is that I will be dealing with what are often complex ideas in a simplified but I trust basically accurate way and, having outlined them, applying some of them in a rather mechanical fashion. This is because I am a firm believer in learning by doing and, given the general aversion to theory, what is important is getting people started by providing them with a few templates that may be readily applied, especially in their more substantive courses. However, what I have also discovered through my own teaching is that, once someone has had some success in using such templates, their confidence grows rapidly, as does the subtlety and the range of their work. The result is that the props provided here may be quickly put to one side, remaining available for use and indeed criticism and revision in moments of crisis. The second 'health warning' is that this book is written from a particular point of view and therefore, although I have tried to cover a wide range of positions and present them accurately, the coverage is not comprehensive and it is quite possible that my own preferences for ordinary realism and neoclassicism may have biased my presentations of alternative positions. This said, one way of determining the success or failure of the book would be to ask if it has helped you to recognize any such bias.

In writing this book I have, of course, incurred many debts to individuals and institutions. First among the individuals to whom I am indebted is Frank Pearce with whom I have enjoyed many years of conversation on matters theoretical. I have also been fortunate enough to have spent time talking theory with Harold Wolpe, Bryan Turner, Paul Sutton, Frank Webster, John Scott, Mick Mann, David Lockwood, Ted Benton, Ian Craib, John Solomos, Kathianne Hingwan, Roger Woodiwiss, Bob Jessop, Jose Lopez, John Holmwood, George Kolankiewicz, Kerry Lee, Garry Potter, Mireille Hebing, Rob Stones, Ali Rattansi, Fehti Acikel, Mersut Ergun, Alan Dawe, Paul Hirst, Nicos Mouzelis, Roy Todd, Rod Broadhurst, and Jen-To Yao. Very special thanks are due to my partner, Aya Tokita, for her illustrations and her patience during my 'absences'. Institutionally, I am greatly indebted to the departments of sociology at Essex and City universities for being true *ateliers*, and to the Department of Sociology of the Chinese University of Hong Kong, and Professors Rance Lee and Stephen Chiu in particular, for providing me with the visiting fellowship that allowed me to begin writing this book. Last but certainly not least, I must thank all those students who have had to listen to me, and try to learn from me, as I have struggled to make sense of the remarkable activity we call social theory – their questions, comments, ideas, and perhaps especially their difficulties, have been, and continue to be, an inspiration.

Note

1   This statement is not quite accurate since books by American authors that purport to do just this have long been available: Stinchcombe (1968), Hage (1972), Hoover and Donovan (2004), Powers (2004) and Shoemaker *et al.* (2004), for example. However, excellent though they may be in their own terms, these terms are rather narrow in that such texts discuss theory only within the context of what seems to me to be a broadly logical positivist conception of the research process (see Chapter 2) and do not seem to be aware that there are other conceptions that have reasonable claims to be considered as equally scientific.

Part One
The Theory of Social Life

1 Visualizing the social

The key to being able to use and contribute to the development of social theory is getting the point. And the key to getting the point is thinking simply, beginning with your understanding of what theory is and does. What I mean by thinking simply is being able to reduce even complex ideas to short summary – and very often descriptive – definitions and statements. These should be easy to remember and should suggest how the looking that they allow may be manipulated. Consider, for example, the following set of interlinked definitions:

> 'theory' consists of words formed into a set of interlinked concepts – change the words and you change the concepts and therefore the theory;

> 'concepts' such as alienation, anomie, class, status, identity, discourse, and conceptions of their links are definitions that have gained their form and content as a consequence of their creators following a particular research strategy – the data so produced are used to give substance to the definitions and therefore as the data develop and/or change so too must the concepts;

> a 'research strategy' is a process of empirical investigation conducted on the basis of a set of assumptions as to what sort of thing society is ('ontological' assumptions) and how one should go about gaining knowledge of it ('epistemological' assumptions) – change either set of assumptions or both and you change the nature of the research strategy and consequently that of the data, the concepts and their linkages too. In addition, where or insofar as such concepts are linked with one another to form an overall theory, a change in any one of them is likely to require a change in some or all of the others.

As the progression of this set of definitions suggests and as will become very clear in the course of the remaining chapters of Part 1, each of these ostensibly simple definitions hides a set of often conflicting views as to the proper way to produce pictures of the social world. However, what is important here is that, given some serious consideration, this set of definitions and the actions they suggest are so simple or obvious that even if you are reading them for the first time you should quickly gain some sense of what the word 'theory' means and therefore of how abstract statements can determine and alter what you can see. As important, remembering such definitions should also prevent you from ever being fazed by such otherwise intimidating terms as concept, ontology, and epistemology, whether you come across them in your reading or have to use them to organize or talk about your own thinking. More than this, the practical import of such definitions can itself be summarized by a simple three-dimensional image, namely that of a telescope and the varying effects of different filters (metatheoretical assumptions) and lenses (concepts) on what you can see.

This image of what theory is and involves is very basic; indeed so basic that, like many of the other things I as the naked practitioner will say, I am almost embarassed to acknowledge its existence. However, the point is not whether or not the image I use is oversimplified or indeed too personal – images of mental processes are always very personal for reasons that are probably best left to psychoanalysts to ponder. Rather, the point is that such images and the definitions they summarize should allow you to work and play creatively with concepts and theories and, given the necessary diligence, produce insightful and sometimes even novel understandings of social life. This is something that is impossible if your definitions are too long or too awkward and your mental picture of their interrelationships is consequently too complex – as the error messages on computers used to say a lot more often in the past than they do now, this is because of 'insufficient memory'.

Taking a closer look at what theory does and how it does it, the idea that social theory is a form of visual work may at first sound strange and even self-contradictory. This is for two reasons. First, for many people the very term 'theory' suggests difficulty, abstraction and opacity rather than the ease, self-evidentness and clarity that we associate with our sense of sight. Second, and again for many people because of the association with difficulty, 'theory' suggests the need for inspiration and even genius rather than something as prosaic as mere work. The premise upon which this book rests is that these senses of theory as anti-visual and/or requiring special qualities of mind on the part of practitioners are the major reasons why many people regard it as excessively and even irritatingly difficult and therefore to be avoided or, failing that, bluffed or blagged. My primary aim in what follows will therefore be to convince you that the conception of theory as anti-visual and 'for geniuses only' is mistaken and that, on the contrary, theory is an everyday part of our visual apparatus and theorizing a skill that can be learned like any other.

Seeing theoretically

The first step towards overcoming any resistance to the idea that theory might be visual work is to understand that even ordinary sight involves not only our eyes but also, minimally, our brains, language, social position and even our political commitments. The result is that what we see, the visual domain, is also the product of far more than our eyes. Thus the world literally looks – sometimes slightly, sometimes very – different depending on, for example, who you are, what mood you are in, your social position, or even the nature of your political or religious beliefs. Hence our talk of 'beauty being in the eye of the beholder', or of optimistic people 'looking at the world through rose-tinted spectacles'; hence also the one thing that everyone knows about the Inuit peoples of North America, namely that they can recognize 40 or more different kinds of snow; and hence, finally, the difference between those who see suicide bombers as terrorists and those who see them as martyrs. The psychologically and sociologically determined nature of vision is therefore something that is well understood in daily life. However, for some reason it often seems very difficult to extend this insight to theory and therefore to regard theory too as simply another example of the way in which something non-visual can alter our perception. This is also surprising because, in their leisure time, at least some of the people who report such difficulty will often very happily resort to non-linguistic means of one kind or another, such as drink or drugs, to alter their perception and so enhance their pleasure. In sum, the puzzle is that a knowledge that is widely possessed in everyday life – the social determination of sight – and that can be used for a purpose that is widely regarded as pleasurable – altering perception – tends to be forgotten or feared where theory is concerned.

There could be many different explanations for this state of affairs, some complex and some insulting, but I am going to bet on a simple one, largely because something can be done about it. Recognizing the social determination of sight and altering our perception by lifting a glass or smoking something requires no special knowledge or skill. However, self-consciously altering one's perception by imbibing or drawing on, so to speak, a theory requires some knowledge and skills that are undoubtedly somewhat recondite even if they require no special qualities of mind. Put briefly, what I intend to do in what follows is to use the pedagogical resource represented by the widely diffused sense that sight is socially determined for the purpose of enhancing your capacity to theorize. As a start, and in order that you quickly gain a sense of the degree to which your sight is already structured by social life and theory, I would suggest that you carry out the following exercises: watch at least the first 20 minutes of John Sayles' wonderful film *Brother from Another Planet;* imagine yourself as the proverbial visitor from Mars, but in this case one who cannot hear or read anything and who has been asked to stand in a busy part of a town or city well known to you and write down what you think it could see – when you have finished writing please refer to note 1 at the end of this chapter to see what you have taught yourself.[1]

In my view, the best of the more formal ways to begin the effort to gain a self-conscious and therefore manipulable understanding of how the words, ideas and data that constitute theory can affect vision and why therefore theory can be regarded as visual work is to take on board the insights contained in some recent contributions to the history and philosophy of art as summarized and developed by Martin Jay (1988). Jay begins by distinguishing between 'vision' (sight as such) and 'visuality' (the kind of intellectually, socially and historically affected or constructed sight discussed above). He moves on to explain how, beginning in the Renaissance, painters started to intervene self-conciously in the process of structuring sight to produce what they regarded as truer and/or more expressive images of real or imagined scenes. And, finally, he makes what is the critical point in the current context, which is that these painterly interventions prefigured, even if they did not necessarily directly influence, various philosophical ideas concerning how the world might best be looked at when seeking knowledge of it.

On this basis Jay distinguishes what he refers to as the three visualities or 'scopic regimes' that constitute the basis of our present array of ways of self-conciously structuring sight, whether as artists or social scientists. According to Jay, there were three such regimes within what is commonly known as classical art. The first is named after the technical advance in painting, perspective, that occurred in the fifteenth century and made such art possible. The significance of the invention of perspective is that it solved a problem that had defeated all previous generations of painters. That problem was how to represent depth or the third dimension. The fact that objects may be taller or shorter or wider or thinner than one another had never caused any problems for painters. However, the fact that objects may be closer to, or further away from, the viewer had completely defeated them until the invention of perspective. What the inventors of perspective discovered was that depth could be represented by converting differences of distance into differences of height and width and constructing the composition around a point that represented the most distant part of the scene, the vanishing point (for descriptions of the instruments they used to help them with this conversion – for example 'Alberti's grid', so-called because it was developed by the great theorist of perspective, Leon Battista Alberti – visit http://www.acmi.net.au/ail/drawing_machines.html). The difference that perspective made may be easily appreciated by contrasting any pre-Renaissance painting (http://www.artcyclopedia.com – search in 'movements') with any Renaissance one (http://www.artcyclopedia.com – search in 'movements' again). Jay calls this regime 'Cartesian perspectivalism' because what the early Renaissance artists had also discovered was that sight had to be manipulated by the intellect if they were to produce an accurate representation of the world. What we see in the world is therefore in part at least a product of our thought about it. And in the same way that the intellectual techniques associated with perspective explain the disposition of images on a canvas so, more generally, and as Rene Descartes was later to argue, human reason in part accounts for what we see in the world. Jay also argues that the sense of distance that perspective produces evokes the same cool, objective and masterful gaze that Descartes later sought as he moved towards formulating what has become known as his *Cogito* (see below, pp. 17–18). Thus Jay ends his discussion of this regime by suggesting that perspectivalism prefigured both rationalism and, later, philosophical idealism.

Jay finds the second scopic regime best exemplified by the domestic scenes common in early seventeenth-century Dutch painting (http://www.artcyclopedia.com – 'picture search' for Jan Vermeer, *Woman Holding a Balance*). Following the art historian Svetlana Alpers (1983), Jay refers to this regime as the 'art of describing'. Of course perspective is deployed but in this case to get closer to the scene – to the objects, people, emotions and social life it represents. For this reason, Jay argues that the 'art of describing' prefigured philosophical empiricism or positivism and may indeed have directly helped to make it possible. The third scopic regime is that instanced above all by late seventeenth-century Baroque painting (http://www.artcyclopedia.com – 'picture search' for Andrea Pozzo, *The Apotheosis of St. Ignazio*). Here the lessons drawn from perspectivalism and the 'art of describing' are combined with mystical ideas about the power of linguistic and mathematical representations (Yates 1979: 25). The result is the creation of an effect which is surrounding, enveloping and overwhelming, and which produces in the viewer a sense of his or her subordination and helplessness in the face of a far greater power, namely God or a temporal absolute monarch. A similar sense of awe, bewilderment and individual finitude was also achieved in a more literary way through the use of classical allegories in other Baroque paintings – allegories achieve such effects because of their power to transport the viewer to other and unfamiliar worlds (Benjamin 1977). The philosophical position most closely associated with such paintings at the time they were produced was Gottfried Wilhelm von Leibniz's 'monadology'; both were aspects of the Baroque or the culture of the Counter-Reformation and the rise of the absolute monarchies of Europe (Maravall 1986). Thus, for example, one consequence of Leibniz's effort to reconcile rationalism with theism in his monadology was his argument that one effect of what is understood as our monadic or singular relation to the world is that we do not realize that we possess free will only in order to carry out God's will; that is, our sense of freedom is final proof of our insignificance. Remarkably, the philosophical position that baroque art prefigured attained its greatest degree of influence some 200 years later in the form of postmodernism (Buci-Glucksmann 1994; Woodiwiss 2001: 143ff.).

To sum up, the relations between the various components of these three scopic regimes may be schematically represented as follows:

Rationalism: *people* produce *images* of *objects*.
Empiricism: *objects* evoke impressions in *people* who produce *images*.
Baroque: *images* produce *objects* in the minds of *people*.

Metatheories and visualities

In a very general sense, the fundamental sources of any theory's pictorial power are the selective or filtering effects of its ontological assumptions concerning what it is being used to look at, and its epistemological assumptions concerning how to go about gaining knowledge of whatever is being looked at. The collective term used to refer to these assumptions is metaphysics, or more commonly these days, metatheory (theory of theory). The reason I use the phrase 'in a very general sense' in talking about the role of these assumptions is because their effect on vision is to specify certain general qualities of what one is looking for or how one thinks one should go about looking for it, rather than to specify what it actually is or how exactly it should be looked for.

To specify metatheoretically and therefore in advance what exactly you are looking at and/or for and how exactly knowledge of it should be pursued would be to render a good part of the research process unnecessary and even fraudulent because the only purpose of research would be to make what had already been decided seem more plausible than might otherwise be the case. Indeed, the only circumstances under which one is justified in making assumptions when one is engaged in the pursuit of knowledge is where one has to take a decision about an issue that is inherently undecidable and that therefore cannot itself be made into a researchable topic. Thus the issues about which you may legitimately make assumptions, that is, make decisions on the basis of your own subjective preferences – the more educated these preferences are the better of course – are very few and relate to what might be described, with just a little hyperbole, as the ultimate mysteries concerning the place of human beings in the universe.

Put in terms that are close to the manner in which such issues are commonly posed in the context of social theory, someone's position *vis-à-vis* the ultimate ontological issues may be uncovered by asking and answering the following questions:

1   Is social life something that depends on us thinking about it for its existence or would it still exist even if we stopped thinking about it? Is it a picture in our minds or is it something picturable in the world?

2   Is social life something that is ultimately material (that is, accessible through our senses) or is it something that is ultimately immaterial (a matter of thought, for example)? Is it something that can be seen or heard, and so forth, or can it only be imagined?

3   Is social life something that ultimately consists of human beings or of other orders of being (structures, for example)? When you think of society, do you see people going about their lives or do you see the following, for example, as things in their own right: states, classes, or ideologies; divisions of labour, *collective consciousnesses*, anomic disjunctions, or suicidogenic currents; epistemes, discourses, or governmentalities?

And their position *vis à vis* the ultimate epistemological issues may be uncovered by asking and answering these questions:

1   In investigating the nature of social life, is it best to begin with observation (interviews or surveys, for example) or in some other way (intuition, hunches, values, conversations, pre-existing theories, for example)?

2   In investigating the nature of social life, is it ever permissible to reason without reference to data or research results? If so, under what conditions?

3   On completing a piece or programme of social research is it ever possible to be *certain* that one knows the truth? If not why not and what confidence can you have in the validity of the work produced?

At this point it will help if you take some time to answer the questions contained in Figure 1.1, which concern the metatheoretical assumptions you bring to the study of social theory. It will help in at least three ways. First, answering these questions should reduce the intellectual anxiety commonly aroused on simply reading or hearing the words 'ontology' and 'epistemology' by showing you that it is quite possible to answer these questions in the absence of much or even any prior study of the issues involved, especially if the answers are attempted late at night with a few kindred spirits and copious amounts of wine and cigarettes. Second, in providing answers you will begin to turn a collection of most likely hitherto haphazardly generated opinions into a coherent set of guiding principles, which you should then be able to master rather than merely learn, because you should now be gaining a practical appreciation of their significance for what and how you look at the social. Third, any difficulty in answering the questions means that their consideration may also function as a self-administered diagnostic test in relation to your level of metatheoretical self-conscious-ness, and indeed self-confidence, with the result that you will discover where you need to do some more thinking.

Ask yourself the following questions and circle 'yes' or 'no' no matter in how many columns it appears in note 2 at the end of the chapter because there are more than three valid or meaningful combinations of answers and you might need to read the key provided below before you finally decide which combination of answers best describes your position.

Ontological questions.
(What sort of thing is being investigated?)

		1	2	3
a)	Does society depend on us thinking about it for its existence?	yes	no	no
b)	Is society a material object (i.e. accessible through our senses)?	no	yes	yes
c)	Does society ultimately consist of individual people? If not what does it consist of?	no/yes	yes	yes/no

Epistemological questions.
(How should society be investigated?)

		1	2	3
a)	Should one begin with observation?	no	yes	no
b)	Should one ever reason without reference to observations?	yes	no	yes
c)	Is certainty possible?		yes (to a degree)	no

Final question.
How would you explain the links between the answers to the ontological questions and the answers to the epistemological ones?

Now refer to note 2 at the end of this chapter in order to find the key that will give a name to your combination of answers.

Figure 1.1 How to identify your own or someone else's metatheoretical position

It is possible to discern five well-established sets of answers within Figure 1.1 and these define the most influential metatheoretical positions (basic picturing systems) within contemporary social theory.[2]

The remaining chapters of Part 1 will discuss and illustrate the consequences of four of these sets of answers in the course of a roughly chronological account of the development of metatheory (a fifth set, that relating to postmodernism, will be discussed in Part 2, see, pp. 125–8 below). This account will necessarily be rather schematic, as indeed will the outlines of the metatheoretical positions that are presented along the way. However, provided that my account and the outlines it contains are accurate, this schematicism should not be the source of problems. Social scientists should be philosophically literate in order that they may competently and effectively use the powerful instruments that metatheoretical assumptions represent. However, they need not be very subtle philosophers because their task is to make broad assumptions work for picturing purposes rather than to explore the intricacies of such assumptions.

Put schematically, the development of metatheory as it relates to contemporary social theory originated in the seventeenth century with two ideas that seemed at the time to be in conflict (the most readable detailed account of this development is contained in Jay 2004: Chapter 2). The first idea was that, given that objects evoke impressions in people who produce images, vision or our sense of sight must provide us with our most trustworthy and reliable means of gaining knowledge. This idea became the basis for the position that we currently know as *empiricism* and its first influential advocate was Sir Francis Bacon. According to Bacon, it should ultimately be possible to derive knowledge of the structure of nature from observations, provided only that one does not allow one's observations to be distorted by obeisance to various idols, namely those associated with tradition (the idols of the tribe), personal idiosyncracies (the idols of the cave), the pursuit of fame (the idols of the market place), and the taking of sides (the idols of the theatre). In sum, Bacon argued that as a result of ever more detailed observation nature may be induced – arrestingly but rather unfortunately given his own participation in torture, he used the term 'tortured' – into giving up its secrets. This is called the method of inductivism.

The second idea was that, on the contrary, given that people produce images of objects, reason (the capacity to think logically or to develop an argument without contradicting oneself) must provide us with our surest means of gaining knowledge. This idea, which became the basis for what we currently know as *rationalism*, was most famously exemplified by Descartes and his *Cogito*. Descartes agreed with Bacon that there are many reasons to doubt that things are what they seem. However, instead of responding to this by developing a system of observational taboos like the doctrine of the idols – that is, by specifying what should be avoided – Descartes responded by pushing scepticism to what he imagined were its limits (some 200 years later the postmodernists were to push it several steps further). An excellent evocation of Descartes' method of 'radical doubt' has been provided by Colin McGinn and, usefully, it is expressed in visual terms:

> ... what you immediately perceive is *always* sense-datum, not the real thing. Therefore you do not directly see physical objects at all but only their representations in the shape of mental sense-data. It is like trying to meet the head of state and only meeting her emissaries. Your direct awareness stops at the level of sense data and does not reach out and catch hold of actual physical objects ... they are not what is immediately before your mind when you have a visual experience. What is immediately before your mind is your mind itself – its current sensory contents ...
>
> When I first encountered this argument I would stare at the furniture around me and try to force my mind to become aware of it, to penetrate the veil of sense-data; but I had the stifling feeling that I was only gazing harder at what was inside me – my own subjective world, not the common public world I had believed in up until then. There was at best a correspondence between the subjective world I was experiencing and the physical world beyond, but there was no way I could step out of my subjective world, to check that the correspondence really held – since I had no direct access to the physical objects that supposedly corresponded to my sense-data. In a way it was like discovering myself to be blind: I couldn't see physical objects! Nor could I touch them, taste them, or smell them. My world had shrunk down to my own conscious self. I was, I suppose, as self-absorbed as many other adolescents, but this was too much. I had lost the world, or rather I had never had it to start with. And from there it only got worse ...
>
> (McGinn 2001: 15–16)

Descartes, however, avoided the terrors that tormented the young McGinn by simultaneously asking whether, after he had called into doubt everything he could, anything remained of which he could be certain. He eventually found such a thing in the knowledge that he was thinking and therefore knew himself to exist. This is the idea summarized as *cogito ergo sum* (I think therefore I am). What Descartes emphasized about his discovery was that it owed nothing to sense perception in that, although he could not see or hear his own thought, he was absolutely certain of its occurrence. Thus the general conclusion he drew was that the pursuit of knowledge was ultimately a matter of using one's reason to discover the invisible structures that produce the appearances that we see. In this way Descartes invented the method of deductivism.

Conclusion

Later in the seventeenth century, the two ideas upon which our contemporary social-theoretical visualities rest – that knowledge is produced either by the senses, principally vision, or by the intellect – were repeated and developed by John Locke and Bishop Berkeley respectively. Berkeley's attempt to combine vision and reason and keep a place for religious faith by making God's intellect the ultimate guarantee of the external world's existence stimulated an extremely powerful and sometimes amusing restatement of the case for vision over reason by the Scottish Enlightenment thinker, David Hume, who ended an imagined discussion with a rationalist as follows:

> Whether your scepticism [as to the independent existence of the external world] be as absolute and sincere as you pretend, we shall learn by and by, when the company breaks up: we shall see whether *you go out at the door or the window.* (Hume [1779] (1990): 132, emphasis added: I am grateful to Frank Pearce for bringing this passage to my attention).

Because of the rigour of his inductivism (the view that reasoning should proceed solely on the basis of observations), Hume insisted that, whereas observation is indeed the method of science, one could never use observations to provide a basis for any understandings of causes. This is because causal relations are invisible and so simply beyond our ken, and anyway observational data are always provisional in that you can never be sure that any of them will be confirmed as true the next time you engage in any observation. However, had Hume's rigorous inductivism been fully accepted by the scientists of the nineteenth century, little if any of the progress they made in understanding the world would have been possible because so much of it involved imagining causal connections and either trying either to validate them or to use such knowledge for practical purposes (Hirst 1975). Nevertheless, and somewhat ironically, the *logic* of Hume's position seemed then, and remains today, incontestable to many social science practitioners as well as philosophers interested in science with the result that they remain haunted by it.

Notes

1 Now look at what you have written and ask yourself the following questions: first, 'Are the words I have used truly purely descriptive of what I have seen, as in such cases as "building", "creatures moving around", etc.?'; second, 'Are any of the words I have used specific to

human culture in general or local cultures in particular, as in such cases as "shop", "office", "factory", "off licence", "liquor store" and "McDonalds"?'; third, 'Are any of the words I have used derived from social theory, as in such cases as "interacting", "working class", "ethnic minority"?' Of course, in 'reality', even the answers given to the first question would be beyond a visitor from another planet. However, notwithstanding this weakness in the design of the exercise, and given that most people who attempt the exercise will have answered the second two questions positively, what it demonstrates is just how taken for granted the influence of cultural and even sociological ideas is on our ways of seeing.

2   *Key*:
1 = Rationalism/idealism; 2 = Empiricism/logical positivism;
3 = Realism.

Where double answers (e.g. no/yes) are given, the first is currently the most common within the tradition.

The three metatheoretical traditions identified in the key are not the only ones to have ever existed but they do comprise the basic ingredients out of which all others have been created. Thus the various interpretivisms and social constructionisms are combinations of an idealist ontology with an empiricist epistemology, and the more sophisticated variants of postmodernism are a combination of a realist ontology with an idealist epistemology.

Rationalism/idealism is a visuality produced by ontologically assuming that society is a mental phenomenon that depends on humans thinking about it (i.e. upon subjective meanings) for its existence, is not material or accessible through our senses, and basically consists of either some sort of suprahuman cultural or spiritual entity such as Hegel's *geist* (spirit) or, in the case of what is known as 'subjective idealism', of an intersubjective community of individual human minds. Therefore, epistemologically, some sort of intuition rather than observation has to be where the process of understanding should start, no moves in an argument should be undertaken without empirical support, but nevertheless certainty may be attained in the end.

Empiricism/logical positivism is a visuality produced by ontologically assuming that society exists whether or not humans think about it, is material and therefore accessible through the senses, and basically consists of individual human beings. Therefore, epistemologically, observation should be where the process of understanding begins, no move in an argument should be made without prior empirical confirmation, and certainty may eventually be approached but only to the degree that such empirical confirmation has been achieved.

Realism is a visuality produced by ontologically assuming that society exists whether or not humans think about it, is material, and basically consists of either individual human beings or *sui generis* social entities sometimes called structures. Therefore, epistemologically, because the gulf between individual minds and external reality is ultimately unsurpassable, theoretical imagination combined with observation to produce models must be where you should begin the process of understanding, moves in an argument or adjustments to a model may sometimes be undertaken without empirical support, and certainty is forever impossible.

Interpretivism is a visuality produced by ontologically assuming that society is a mental phenomenon that depends on humans thinking about it (i.e. upon subjective meanings) for its existence, is not material and yet is accessible to our senses in that it basically consists of an intersubjective community of individual human minds of which all humans are a part. Therefore, epistemologically, because as human beings we are both part of what we study and externally visible and so accesssible through our senses, empathetic understanding should be supported by observation, no move in an argument should be made prior to its empirical confirmation, and certainty may be approached but only to the degree that such empirical confirmation has been achieved. *Social constructionism*, which unfortunately is often confused with postmodernism these days, is a present-day variant of subjective idealism that emerged as a critique of interpretivism in that it shares the same ontological stance but epistemologically reasserts the idealist tradition's belief in the sufficiency of empathetic or, sometimes, conversational understanding.

Postmodernism, as exemplified by thinkers such as Jean Baudrillard, is a visuality produced by ontologically assuming that society exists whether or not humans think about it, is material, and basically consists of *sui generis* mental or cultural entities usually called discourses. However, epistemologically, because the process through which discourses construct the social is invisible, theoretical imagination rather than observation must be where the process of understanding should start. Moves in an argument therefore may be undertaken without empirical support, and certainty is a personal matter.

How to criticize the present author: I would answer as a straight-down-the-line realist for whom structures rather than people are the primary object of sociological enquiry. Thus you could begin to unravel the argument presented in Part 2 by simply disagreeing with any one or more of my answers to the metatheoretical questions and drawing out the consequences. (For more on how to make a critique and construct an alternative, see below p. 156.)

2   Looking for laws

In an effort to exorcise Hume's ghost, a group of philosophers in the 1920s formed what became known as the Vienna Circle (Collins 1998: Chapter 13). The Circle's members were by-and-large committed to trying to reconcile Hume's insistence on the epistemological privileging of vision with the actual achievements of the natural sciences. To cut a rather long and complicated story very short indeed, what the Circle did was to specify how the metatheoretical assumptions of empiricism could be operationalized and a set of protocols for, or a template as to how research should be carried out, could be created. Retrospectively, and ignoring the particularities of the various contributors, this template was produced by combining the metatheoretical assumptions contained in column 2 of Figure 1.1 with data culled from the history of the natural sciences. Thus, the ontological assumptions basic to the empiricist tradition – that the world exists independently of our thought about it, is material and therefore accessible through our senses, and consists of things whose precise nature varies with the science involved – were regarded as confirmed. So too were the implied epistemological corollaries (ideas that necessarily follow) of these ontological assumptions: observation is essential not only for research to begin but also throughout the process because, given that the world is not a mental projection, there is no other way of rationally or logically investigating whatever exists within it. The only epistemological issue that remained unclear was the one relating to the degree of confidence that could be placed in the truthfulness of any law produced on this basis. For a time certainty was thought possible but gradually, in deference to the spectre of Hume as well as because of the sheer difficulty of the enterprise, and encouraged by the prestige already long enjoyed by probability theory and statistics, the establishment of high degrees of probability was thought to be sufficient to justify talking of laws, and indeed to be a more 'scientific' formulation.

In all this the philosophers of the Vienna Circle, or the logical positivists as they became known, were confirming not just Hume's ghostly presence but also his logic, except that what they had learnt from the history of science was that there was more to science than observation. More particularly, what they had learned was that there was more to reason's role in science than simply justifying the primacy of observation. This was because reason or logic was necessary, albeit in combination with observation, for the creation of classification systems, the formulation of hypotheses and tests, the interpretation of test results, the formulation of laws, and indeed the working out of the consequences for observation of any laws, no matter how provisional – hence the labelling of the Vienna Circle's position as *logical* positivism.

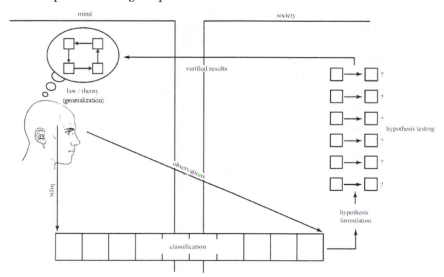

Figure 2.1 Empiricism/logical positivism

The template for the research process so constructed, which will be referred to hereafter as the final or empiricist template, is represented in Figure 2.1. Empiricism's ontological assumptions are pictured spatially by the separate squares representing mind and visible matter and the gap between them, which together provide the background to Figure 2.1. The consequences for research strategy are pictured as the flow diagram in the foreground. Thus what I will call the 'final template' represents the research process or theory-making as requiring five phases, which are understood as a 'hypothetico-deductive' loop in that they are to be continuously repeated until the gap between mind and matter (social life in the present case) has been overcome. These five phases are:

1   Observing the phenomena of interest.
2   Classifying the observations made so as to provide a bridge between the mind and the external world by distinguishing the

different entities or qualities (variables) and processes present and/
or operating within the phenomena being observed.

3 Formulating hypotheses as to the nature of any such entities or
   qualities (variables), processes and the relations between them.

4 Formulating and carrying out experimental tests of any such
   hypotheses.

5 Formulating and formalizing laws on the basis of the aggregation
   of the confirmed hypotheses.

What makes the process into a loop is not simply that hypothesis formulation and testing are repeated and repeated until any proposed laws
have been securely established but also that, once any law has been even
only very provisionally established, it is used deductively to guide the subsequent observing, classifying, hypothesizing and testing. What makes this
process an instance of a constructed visuality, albeit a minimalist variant,
rather than an exercise in simple vision is, of course, that, like the work of
Alpers' Dutch painters (see above, p. 13), observation is governed by reason
in the form of explicit and self-consciously produced rules.

Nothing in philosophy, or science for that matter, remains 'final' for
very long and what ultimately also became known as the *hypothetico-deductive approach* or the *covering law model* was quickly subjected to criticisms
and revisions. Initially these were restricted to the rejection of the repre-
sention of the research process as a machine for mechanically grinding out
'iron laws'. Thus, without challenging the basic design of the template,
highly influential figures such as Karl Popper (1963) argued that scientific
research is a more subtle, tentative and provisional affair than the template
acknowledges. More specifically, he and others argued that the template
should be revised to take account of the role of intuition or theoretically
derived 'conjectures' in the research process, to recognize that the proper
role of hypothesis formulation and experimental testing is not the verifica-
tion of possible laws but the attempt to prove any supposed laws false
(falsificationism), and to emphasize that laws are statements characterized
by high levels of probability (degrees of likeliness) rather than by absolute
certainty.

In time, the criticisms of the final model became much more radical.
Before outlining these criticisms and their consequences in terms of reviving older, albeit hither to undifferentiated, alternative models of the
research process and therefore understandings of the nature of theory too,
something should be said about the significance of empiricism for social
theory. This is that empiricism has been much more significant in relation
to the understanding of social life than most non-positivist social theorists
have acknow-ledged. The unacknowledged character of the empiricist contribution is demonstrated by the fact that social theory textbooks very
seldom if ever contain discussions of empiricist social theory, which, in

turn, may make my suggestion of its significance sound rather startling. To my mind, this neglect of empiricist social theory is a product of the basic problem with current textbooks in social theory that this text is an attempt to overcome, namely the assumption that theory can be understood independently of the research process. Because of this assumption, discussion of the significance of empiricism in the production of knowledge of the social is restricted to methods textbooks where, given empiricism's historical association with statistics, it is most often presented as providing the rationale behind certain quantitative techniques, rather than as a research strategy which has as its goal the formulation of an overarching social theory in the form of the discovery of an interconnected set of probabilistic social laws.

The American empiricist tradition

Another reason for this neglect is that, sadly, no instance exists of a finished set of sociological laws and their associated concepts. Moreover, the laws that have been proposed may be characterized, depending on one's point of view, as instances of either heroic or foolish endeavour because of the contrast between the enormous amount of effort necessary for their production and what appears to many non-empiricists to be the triviality of their content. My favourite example is the 'S theory' produced in the 1940s by one of America's most committed sociological empiricists, Stuart Carter Dodd. This is Jennifer Platt's description of Dodd's 'S theory':

> The theory tells little of what relationships to expect between phenomena.
>   One cannot solve for unknowns from it without further data … It takes whatever data the observer records, good, bad, or indifferent, and describes in definite symbols the operational degree of precision of those data, tells how they may be classified, and prepares them in standardized and parsimonious form ready for further manipulation to discover deeper relationships in those data. The function of the theory is thus, largely, to improve methodology systematically, more than to immediately state a system of generalizations about the behaviour of social phenomena. The system developed is one in which symbols are provided for twelve basic concepts, whose permutations '… will be shown to define by formulat more than four hundred derived concepts which summarize and comprehensively classify quantitative societal phenomena' … The symbols used are T for time, I for indicators of the societal residue of characteristics of people and their environments, L for length, P for populations, plus those for the operators adding, subtracting, multiplying, dividing, aggregating, cross-classifying,

correlating and identifying, and various exponents and scripts specifying the kind and number of classes, class-intervals and cases of what the index denotes. This leads to formulae such as this, which is one of those Dodd offers as examples:

$$S_3 = \underline{a{:}z_t}\ T\text{-}1{:}(P_1\ P_{11}^{-1}\ T^{-1})$$

(That summarizes a table showing the changes over time in the ratio of marriages to divorces.) The 'quantic formula', derived from the T I L P description, gives the 'quantic number' which: serves to classify every S [any quantifiable social phenomenon] that can exist into a single, definite, unambiguous category according to its combination of indices and exponents. The quantic number thus provides a thoroughgoing basis of classification for all quantifiable societal phenomena ...

(Platt 1996: 80–1)

Despite the neglect encouraged by such efforts, the fact remains that we owe much of what we know about social life to empiricism, thanks to the governmental gathering of information in the form of the stat(e)istics and the surveys that empiricism initially encouraged and legitimated (Abrams 1968). Also, today, and more ambiguously, it is not possible to make sense of much of what happens in American departments of sociology, and indeed of many of the articles in American sociology journals, unless the existence of the empiricist research programme is assumed (on the restricted nature of any direct links between the Vienna Circle and home-grown American empiricism, see Platt 1996: Chapter 13). Given that it can be safely assumed that the formulation of S theory and the like is not at the centre of all this continuing effort, what is? The answer is something called 'middle-range theory'. The production of such theory became the core of American sociological activity in the 1960s, thanks to the legendary common sense and immense prestige of the man who invented the phrase, Robert K. Merton. For Merton (1968: 5), 'theories of the middle range' are 'logically interconnected conceptions which are limited and modest in scope, rather than all-embracing and grandiose.' Their role is to bridge the gap between the 'minor working hypotheses' spawned in abundance in the course of research and the comprehensive speculations that comprise a 'master conceptual scheme'.

In practice, and as is currently still recommended in such American introductory texts as those by Hoover and Donovan (2004), Powers (2004) and Shoemaker *et al.* (2004), efforts to produce middle-range theory typically take the form of quantitative studies of the co-variation (relationships) between small numbers of variables (measurably varying attributes of individual human beings such as age, years of education, income, health), which are taken as proxies for social-structural elements and/or processes. The justification is that, when the numbers of cases and the correlations or regressions (apparent interrelationships) between variables are strong enough, such studies are thought to have significance for understanding causal relationships (Ragin 1994: Chapter 6). One problem resulting from this approach is that the meaning of the word 'theory' appears to have been transformed so that it has come to mean a series of discrete, so-called 'laws' or frequently confirmed hypotheses such as the 'eighteen testable laws for sociology' itemized in Powers (2004). Examples of such laws are:

> **Anger Principle:** other things being equal, anger increases in magnitude as a function of the degree to which actual outcomes fall short of expected outcomes.

> **Conflict/Cohesion Principle:** other things being equal, cohesion within groups increases as a function of the degree of conflict between groups.

> **Principle of Social Control:** other things being equal, the more integrated the members of a group or community are (the more interconnected they are and the more bound they are to common set of beliefs and the fewer offsetting ties people have to other groups or communities), then the greater level of social control the group or community will exert over its members.

> **Principle of Evolution:** other things being equal, the smaller subpopulations are and the less contact they have with each other, the more rapidly and more dramatically they will differentiate from each other.

> **Principle of Intergroup Antagonism:** other things being equal, the greater the level of inequality between groups, the greater the homogeneity within groups, the more substantial the barriers to mobility between groups, and the greater the level of intergroup competition over scarce resources, then the more likely members of both groups are to have a sense of distinct identity and the more profound intergroup tensions will be.

> **Principle of Violent Conflict:** other things being equal, the more recurrent and procedurally regulated conflict is, the less likely it is to turn violent.

Principle of Socialization: other things being equal, socialization is most likely to be effective to the degree that the person being socialized (a) depends on the socializing agent, (b) trusts the socializing agent, and (c) has an opportunity to act out or practice new norms and roles with peers.

(Powers 2004: 223–7)

Although the studies associated with the development and confirmation of such 'laws' often involve the display of very high levels of statistical sophistication and are sometimes theoretically inspired, in the manner of Popper's 'conjectures', they are very seldom 'logically interconnected', whether with a 'master conceptual scheme' or with other such studies. Thus, for those committed to the empiricist project, the results are almost as disappointing as they are risible to empiricism's opponents.

Because of their antithetical metatheoretical assumptions, the latter tend to regard such supposed laws as tautological in the sense that the 'principles' or laws involved merely restate the initial conditions described. Consider the 'Principle of Violent Conflict', for example, which seems to be saying that if violence is prevented for a long time it is less likely to happen! Tragically, one only has to think of recent events the territory of former Yugoslavia to falsify an hypothesis. More generally, non-empiricists even so doubt that variables relating to the attributes of persons can ever be taken as anything more than suggestive but very rough proxies for social-structural elements and processes as, for example, when income or occupation are taken as standing for class (for a discussion of some of the problems this causes, see below pp. 130–6). For a committed empiricist like Hubert Blalock, on the other hand, the widespread adoption of Merton's strategy has turned out to be a missed opportunity of mammoth proportions and one that occurred largely because of what he judges to be the poor quality of the graduate students who produced, and still produce, much of the middle-range theory:

> students lack both the inclination and prior training needed to pursue any theoretical topic in depth. When they search for 'relevant' theory they may indeed come up with a list of theoretical propositions suited for rough translation into a testable research hypotheses but the logical (or mathematical) structure in the underlying theoretical arguments is of little concern to them. In effect they are taught to apply an empirical approach to theoretical arguments, namely to conduct a literature review so as to come up with an eclectic set of researchable questions. In Merton's (1968) terms, they may be concerned with 'empirical generalizations' but not their logical or causal interconnections. When causal diagrams are presented and when path coefficients are

attached to these diagrams, for example, these are rarely accompanied by any kind of thorough discussion of the underlying theory,
the latent or theoretical variables that have been omitted or only
imperfectly measured, or concerns about generalizability or problems of measurement comparability. In short, causal models are
treated in the same perfunctory manner as are serious efforts to
construct verbal theories.

(Blalock 1994: 32)

Reading this passage, it is difficult not to be reminded of the old adage
about bad workmen blaming their tools. However, as well as providing an
illustration of the emotion sometimes attached to theoretical work, especially when one's hopes have been disappointed, the terms of Blalock's criticisms make it clear that for him, as for many others, consolation may be
found in the fact that these hopes have been revived in the form of what is
today called 'formal theory' (Hage 1994; Berger and Zelditch 2002). 'Formal
theory' is a more inclusive project than empiricism in that it allows the
respectability of certain 'verbal theories' such as neo-institutionalism (see
below, p. 121) and rational choice theory. However, it still primarily refers
to the empiricist project and its protagonists repeat Blalock's demand
for the more widespread availability of the right kind of researchers and
students for it to be turned into reality. As Jonathan Turner has put it:

Some of the most creative formal theorizing in sociology currently
comes from organized research programs where scholars at a university or relatively small set of universities conduct research and
train students within a narrow theoretical tradition. Such efforts
produce on a more miniscale the conditions for successful cumulation of knowledge – that is, excluding the lay public and competing knowledge producers, consolidating control over reputation
credits and resources, fostering mutual dependence, and lowering
task uncertainty over what is important.

    The best exemplar of this approach is the development of
'expectation states' theory at Stanford University (e.g., Berger and
Zelditch 1985; Berger, Wagner, and Zelditch 1989). As a prestigious
university, Stanford can recruit and place high-quality students who
then can continue to recruit and place further cohorts of students.
Over time, this process has created a relatively dispersed but intellectually dense network of scholars at prestigious universities.

(Turner 1994: 177)

In other words, the only way finally to realize the potential of the empiricist and/or wider formal theory project is to bring a new level of labour

discipline to the process of theory production and make the right people do the right things.

Conclusion

Although, for reasons that will be discussed in Part 2, the 'middle-range' and 'formal theory' projects have been most influential in the United States, they should not be regarded as either the only approaches within American sociology or as solely American phenomena. Despite the undoubted dominance of these approaches in the United States, all the other approaches discussed below have their supporters there too. Also, at the behest of agencies such as Britain's Economic and Social Research Council (ESRC), research centres with empiricist remits have multiplied in Western Europe since around the mid-1980s. For example, very similar arguments to Turner's for yet more such centres have recently been made in Britain (Commission on the Social Sciences 2003: 118). However, American-style sociological empiricism has never, or at least has not yet, gained the grip on the British or wider European sociological imaginations that it has had in the United States. The result is that not only has the omnipresence of the 'middle-range' project been avoided, but also the data gathered by survey research centres and the sophisticated statistical analysis associated with them are most often, but not without difficulty or costs in terms of coherence, combined with or incorporated into research programmes that rest on metatheoretical assumptions other than those that have been defined here as empiricist (for an excellent example of such work, see Marshall *et al.*, 1989; and see below, pp. 133–4).

3 Looking at models

As its ideas became influential, the Vienna Circle attracted the involvement of several scholars who were either already critical of the Circle's metatheoretical convictions or gradually became so. The most influential amongst such people turned out to be the philosopher Ludwig Wittgenstein and, later, the historian of science Thomas Kuhn. The net effect of their work was to breathe new life into two metatheoretical positions that most members of the Circle must have thought had been rendered anachronistic by the rise of logical positivism. These positions were those we know today as *realism* and *interpretivism/social constructionism*, and by the late 1970s they had displaced logical positivism in the competition for the allegience of most of those interested in 'verbal theory'. Realism, which will be outlined in the present chapter, understands reason to involve much more than logic and argues for a greatly expanded role for reason in the research process. By contrast, today's interpretivism/social constructionism, which will be outlined in the following chapter, insists on the importance for social science of a different kind of observation to that practised in the natural sciences, sometimes to the extent that such observation is thought to rule out the need for theory altogether.

As will be demonstrated by the accounts of Marx and Durkheim's research strategies to be provided below, realism has provided a basis for social-theoretical picturing for a long time. However, it only became a self-consciously articulated position in the 1970s, which means that it is now possible to reclassify certain thinkers who were previously considered to be materialists, empiricists, or even idealists. Marx neither spelt out his metatheoretical assumptions at all fully or systematically, nor imagined that there could be more than one truly scientific approach to the pursuit of knowledge (Althusser 1969; Carver 1975). Although Durkheim (1985) did spell out his assumptions in a systematic fashion, for a long time they were mistaken for those of empiricism by most of his readers including himself (Gane 1988; Stedman-Jones 2001), again because of the absence of an at all precise understanding of the nature of scientific method in the nineteenth century. Of course there were strong disagreements over the accuracy of particular understandings of the method but no serious disagreements concerning its existence and its role in guiding scientific practice. This inchoate consensus only began to break down once the Logical Positivists announced that they finally knew what the scientific method was, because there was now a substantive template that could be examined, criticized, revised and even replaced.

A more specific factor affecting and limiting the past visibility of what is now distinguished as realism is something that is obvious if you compare columns 2 and 3 in Figure 1.1. This factor is that realism shares its ontological assumptions with empiricism in that the world is understood to exist entirely independently of the mind as well as to the material and therefore access-ible through the senses. The only point of ontological difference apparent in Figure 1.1 is that, as far as the study of social life is concerned, realists have been more willing than empiricists to countenance the possibility that social things other than human beings exist and may therefore be theoretically and empirically pictured. As will be explained below, this willingness is what explains the rather striking epistemological differences between the two positions. For the present, however, the point is that, before these epistemological differences were made explicit, the sharedness of ontological assumptions meant that realism and empiricism were indistinguishable from one another. Indeed, until very recently, realism was simply thought of as a component of empiricism, as a way of specifying the perceptual consequences of its ontological assumptions, namely that objective vision or looking is both possible and essential.

I will now move on to outline how the 'naive realism' just described was transformed into 'ordinary realism' or what Roy Bhaskar (1978) dubbed 'scientific realism' and, referring to Figure 3.1, how therefore the same ontology came to be combined with a very different epistemology as compared to that of empiricism – an epistemology that argued for substantive theory over observation as the beginning of the research process, for a continuing and independent role for substantive theory as opposed to 'pure' logic in that process, as well as for the unsurpassability of the gulf between mind and society and therefore the utter fallibility of any theory, no matter how well made it might be. The story of this transformation is a surprising one in that it was a rather definitely unintended consequence of the critiques of logical positivism made by the two deviant members of the Vienna Circle mentioned earlier, Wittgenstein and Kuhn. By the 1970s, and notwithstanding his Austrian origins, Wittgenstein was widely regarded by mainstream Anglo–American analytical philosophers as having been the single most influential philosopher of the twentieth century. This was thanks largely to his work on language and meaning, concerning which

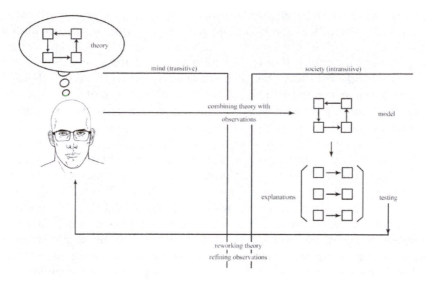

Figure 3.1 Realism

he produced two diametrically opposed theories. One, a product of his youthful precocity, was presented in his book *Tractatus Logicus Philosophicus* (1922), where he argued that words gain their meanings as a result of them being taken as pictures of things or actions in the world. This conception of language played a significant role in the emergence of logical positivism, because it suggested the possibility of the objective description of the world which, in turn, justified the privileged position alloted to observation in the pursuit of knowledge. To the considerable and understandable discomfort of his colleagues in the Circle, Wittgenstein later rejected this conception altogether and proposed a new account of the nature of language, which was set out in in his posthumously published *Philosophical Investigations* (1963). According to this new account, words gain their meanings not from the things and actions to which they refer, but from the ways in which they are used; that is, they gain their meanings not from the world external to the mind but from the interaction between the mind and the external world. Far from being supportive of logical positivism, this new conception of language very seriously undermined it since because the inherent variability of language use implies an equal variability in meaning and therefore the impossibility of objective linguistic description.

Moreover, it proved possible for later philosophers to draw out the implications of this new understanding of the nature of language in at least two very different ways. On the one hand, it was frequently argued that words derive their meanings almost entirely from the purposes they serve. This was the position that ultimately led to the atheoretical subjective idealism brought to sociology and lucidly exemplified by Peter Winch, whose contribution to social constructionism will be discussed in the following chapter. On the other, it was occasionally argued that words, including those that are used to form scientific concepts, have practical significance because they accurately, if only ever partially, grasp the true nature of the external world. This was the position that eventually led to scientific realism when it provided the basis for a similarly deviant or contrarian reading of Kuhn's incredibly influential book, *The Structure of Scientific Revolutions* (1970).

What Kuhn did in his book was to challenge the account of the history of natural science that was both assumed and implied by the logical positivists' conception of the research process. Taking a broadly social-historical approach rather than one narrowly focused on the history of scientific ideas, Kuhn paid attention to the wider context in which such ideas had developed and especially to the structure and dynamics of scientific communities. His principal and highly subversive conclusions were: first, that what he terms 'normal science' begins for its practitioners not with observation, but with socialization into governing 'paradigms' or particular ways and means of looking at and manipulating the pertinent aspects of nature; and second, that these paradigms do not change, *à la* Popper, gradually and incrementally as adjustments are made in the light of falsified hypotheses, but quite suddenly and radically when it is realized that nothing short of an intellectual revolution can prevent a continuing and increasingly scandalous failure to acknowledge an accumulation of negative findings that can no longer be explained away.

Kuhn summarizes the ontological consequences of his investigations in the following highly ambiguous passage:

> Examining the record of past research from the vantage point of contemporary historiography, the historian of science may be tempted to exclaim that when paradigms change, the world itself changes with them. Led by a new paradigm, scientists adopt new instruments and look in new places. Even more important, during revolutions scientists see new and different things when looking with familiar instruments in places they have looked before. It is rather as if the professional community had been suddenly transported to another planet where familiar objects are seen in a different light and are joined by unfamiliar ones as well. Of course, nothing of quite that sort does occur: there is no geographical transplantation; outside the laboratory everyday affairs usually continue as before. Nevertheless, paradigm changes do cause scientists to see the world of their research-engagement differently. In so far as their only recourse to that world is through what they see and do, we may want to say that after a revolution scientists are responding to a different world.

It is as elementary prototypes for these transformations of the scientist's world that the familiar demonstrations of a switch in visual gestalt prove so suggestive. What were ducks in the scientist's world before the revolution are rabbits afterwards.

(Kuhn 1970: 110)

Unsurprisingly, two very different readings of the significance of Kuhn's work subsequently emerged. The first and very much the majority reading concluded, in line with what was taken to be Wittgenstein's argument, that the world gains its meaning from language rather than vice versa, and that Kuhn had demonstrated that the world changes depending on how one looks at it. It therefore considered him to have advanced a radically interpretivist or social constructionist case (see the discussion of Winch below, pp. 65–8). On the other hand, the minority reading concluded, in line with the contrarian reading of Wittgenstein's argument (words are useful because they are capable of at least partially grasping the true nature of the external world), that what Kuhn had in fact demonstrated was simply that paradigms, and the meanings they summarize, change as we come to understand the world better. This was the reading that eventually resulted in the transformation of naive realism into a self-conscious metatheoretical position, thanks largely to the work of Roy Bhaskar, especially his first book, *A Realist Theory of Science* (1978).

This is how Bhaskar reads what he regards as Kuhn's discoveries as confirming the truth of ontological realism rather than requiring its rejection:

Why do these phenomena portend such disquiet for philosophy? Their acknowledgement sunders the constitutive relation of classical philosophy between subject and object, humans and their universe which interlocks, intertwines and interdefines thought and things. It shatters, in a single double-edged stroke, the isomorphism classical philosophy would establish, in an (empirical or conceptual) anthroporealism, between knowledge and being, as social cognitions and natural phenomena are coupled, drawn together and finally fused in the concepts of the empirical or rational worlds. (No longer can thought be conceived as a mechanical function of given things, as in empiricism; nor can the activity of creative subjects continue to be seen as constituting a world of objects, as in idealism; nor is some combination of the two possible. In short, it becomes mandatory to make the distinction between the (relatively) unchanging real objects which exist outside and perdure independently of the scientific process and the changing (and theoretically-imbued) cognitive objects which are produced within science as a function and result of its practice; that is, between the intransitive and transitive objects of scientific knowledge, and accordingly between the intransitive and transitive dimensions in the philosophy of science.

(Bhaskar 1986: 51)

Put more simply and in a less compressed way, Bhaskar's argument has three parts. First, the occurrence of scientific revolutions disproves the rationalist ontological assumption that nature depends on human minds for its existence, for if this were so these minds could never be outwitted with the result that, for example, experiments would never fail for other than technical reasons. Second, the dependence of 'normal science' on paradigms that require the use of particular theories, methods and even standards of proof disproves the empiricist epistemological assumption that simple observation could ever be sufficient even to begin the process of scientific inquiry. Third and as a consequence, the assumptions that survive Kuhn's critique and provide the basis for a new metatheory are empiricism's ontological realism and rationalism's epistemological assumption that reason and its theoretical products are the *sine qua non* of scientific inquiry. It is the operationalization of this combination that achieved the transformation of naive realism into scientific realism. And it is the fact that this combination defines a research strategy and a way of making theory that is very different to those associated with rationalism and empiricism and that, in turn, confirms that scientific realism is no mere barren hybrid but provides the basis for productive visualities whose distinctiveness had previously been unacknowledged:

> And so science displays a four-phase pattern of development, in which it identifies a range of epistemic phenomena; constructs explanations for them; empirically tests its explanations; leading to the identification of the responsible generative mechanism; which now moves centre stage as the newly-identified phenomena to be explained.
>
> Note that the model-building of the second phase must normally draw upon cognitive resources not already employed in the description of the object (mechanism) in question if it is to count as an 'explanation'. And that such work is seldom simply 'the free creation of our minds, the result of an almost poetic intuition', but proceeds under definite protocols of analogical and metaphorical reasoning and is subject to the contextually variable weight imposed by considerations of consistency, coherence, plausibility, relevance, non-redundancy, independence (novelty), comprehensiveness, depth, fertility, empirical testability, formalisability, geometric or iconic representability, as well as others of a semi-aesthetic kind, such as elegance.
>
> (Bhaskar 1986: 61–2)

This makes scientific realism the basis for a much more elaborate visuality than empiricism, because research, as an inescapably social activity, does not begin with either observation or reason alone but with whatever substantive theory already exists, which is then combined with further, often critical, thoughts and additional observations (see Figure 3.1). Moreover, realism counts a far wider range of materials as observations than empiricism – that is, not only the observer's own but also those made by other investigators, and social actors themselves (Woodiwiss 2001: 54) are regarded as legitimate data. This is because the purpose of such theorizing is not to produce exact and 'pure' experimental data that will allow the discovery of fundamental laws but instead to produce plausible models of whatever aspects of the world its practitioners are interested in. Such models are then used to generate explanations of worldly occurrences, which are tested or, perhaps better, assessed for their adequacy in the light of further data. Finally, the results of these assessments are used to reformulate the theory with which the research began, and the whole process is repeated. Again, as in the case of Logical Positivism, the research process is conceived of as a loop, only in this case it is assumed that it must run forever or until it breaks because it no longer makes sense of the world and is replaced by another differently produced loop, which it is also assumed will run for ever or until it too fails to make sense of the world. The reason why the research process is understood to be never ending is because of the ultimately unsurpassable independence of the world relative to the mind and the consequently very substantial dependence of any theory on the theorist's imagination. Thus, although scientists may be confident that they are undoubtedly picturing something, there is simply no way in which they can ever be certain that they are accurately picturing whatever it is they are interested in:

> Scientists wish to give an accurate theoretical description of reality. It is an open question how much of reality is in fact open to scientific investigation, but scientists must aim at the true characterization of the world. Some theories may already be true, others may have to be modified, and still others may have to be given up completely. One of the ironies of [realist] epistemology is that we are not often in a position to know which is which … knowledge can go hand in hand with doubt … Uncertainty about reality does not show that reality is inaccessible.
>
> (Trigg 1981: 63–4)

There is, then, a tension at the heart of what from now on I will again refer to simply as realism – a tension between its power as a visuality that from the very beginning of the research process can readily produce clear and quite detailed images of the nature of the world and its most basic ontological assumption concerning the independent existence of the world itself, which means that such images must be eternally fallible. This is a tension that makes research not only effective, but also a process that is fraught with temptations and dangers. The temptations include: forgetting that the production of theories and models cannot be a substitute for research but indeed are only justified when they are part of a research project or programme; forgetting that such theories and models must retain forever their status as nominal or imaginary constructs, even when there appears to be a strong research-based possibility that they may be accurate; thinking that the inherent fallibility of all knowledge claims means that one can be careless and self-indulgent in making such claims on the unspoken grounds that if what is correct cannot be known nor can what is wrong.

The most obvious danger arising from succumbing to these temptations is imagining that one can explain the world by producing abstract theories and models alone. An even greater danger is thinking that one can explain the world by elaborating what has been referred to as a 'rich and complex ontology'. The latter phrase is at least oxymoronic and probably self-contradictory, given the intellectual restraint that metatheoretical speculation requires as a condition of its legitimacy (see above, p. 14). What therefore makes this an even greater danger is that it has also been forgotten that the richness and complexity of realist modelling is not the product of its ontological assumptions (which are the properly minimal and substantively mute ones specified in column 3 of Figure 1.1) but of the presence of substantive theory throughout the research process instead of simply at the end, as in the case of non-Popperian empiricist modes of research – theory that, however and to repeat, is a facilitator of models and explanations but which cannot substitute for further research that tests such models.

To my mind, the danger of substituting speculation for research is so great that it renders unacceptable any attempts to turn ordinary realism into a substantive theory of society in its own right, including that made by Bhaskar himself when he went on to develop the position that has become known as critical realism (Woodiwiss 2001: 18). This is because, first, it is difficult to imagine how one could reasonably move from a set of very general scopic rules for looking at society to a single theorization of what is seen. And second, any such move would simply transform a temptation into an inevitability that would once again make realism a position that no sophisticated person would want to embrace – not this time because it is naive but because, in an unfortunate irony, it appears to be just as likely to encourage religious speculation as to encourage research (Bhaskar 2000; Archer *et al.* 2004).

Marx: picturing capitalism

It appears clear in retrospect that Marx and Durkheim, formerly considered to have been a materialist and a positivist respectively, produced their very differently focused pictures of capitalist society on the basis of a realist conception of science. Thus in Marx's case, he began his own project with two influential, pre-existing bodies of theory, those associated with rationalistic idealist German Hegelianism and British political economy, which aspired at least to base itself on empiricist assumptions. Like Bhaskar and others 140 years later, Marx thought that empiricism and rationalism might complement one another in that each might provide at least something of what the other lacked. In Marx's case, political economy provided the role for vision and the empirical knowledge of what, in his *Theses on Feuerbach* (1845), Marx termed 'human sensuous activity', while Hegelianism provided the role for reason and the sense of historical movement that political economy lacked. More specifically, realization of this complementarity had earlier prompted Marx, in the *Economic and Philosophical Manuscripts* (1844), to use Hegel's account of the 'master/slave dialectic' to begin to make some sense of the disgust he had felt on realizing that the political economists did not feel it necessary to inquire into the causes of the inequality whose consequences in the market place so interested them and instead merely referred to it as the result of the 'lottery of life'. According to Hegel, masters necessarily showed no interest in the thoughts and feelings of their slaves, because to do so would involve recognizing the humanity of people who were otherwise treated as things, and therefore, without realizing it, encouraging the slaves to reclaim their humanity and reject their bondage. And this, in turn, would expose the fact that, despite appearances to the contrary, the master was more dependent on the slave than vice versa. Inspired by this idea, as many other social scientists have been since, Marx found the cause of inequality in something that the political economists could not afford to think about because the power of their patrons depended on it. Thus he identified the cause of inequality under capitalism as the monopolization of property in the means of production by the few at the expense of the many. The result of this monopolization of ownership was that the many were thereby alienated or separated from the means to support themselves with the result that when they worked they worked for others and thereby enriched the few owners rather than themselves. Moreover, what Marx hoped was that on learning the truth of their condition the dispossessed, like Hegel's slaves, would rise up, throw off their chains and so both expose the fragility of bourgeois rule and transform society.

In this way, and largely through reading the works of other thinkers, Marx established a distinctive but only partially self-conscious metatheoretical starting point for himself as regards thinking about society:

ontologically, he explicitly assumed that existence (how we live) determines consciousness (what we think) rather than the other way round, which was what the rationalist tradition up to and including Hegel had thought because, as Marx commented, theirs was a visuality that took the primitive form of a *camera obscura* and therefore produced images that were upside down. Marx also explicitly assumed that what existed was material. These are clearly both realist positions. The remainder of Marx's metatheoretical position, including his entire epistemology and his conception of the research process, was never made explicit. Consequently, the nature of this remainder has to be worked out on the basis of his practice. Implicit though much of it may have been, Marx's new metatheory promised from the beginning to provide a new picture of social life. Hegel had argued that the spirit of history or culture made individuals what they were. The political economists had argued that, economically at least, individuals made society what it was. And Marx argued that the economy had made both culture and individuals what they were. All this is set out in the three pages of the *Theses on Feuerbach*. What is not set out in the *Theses* is how the economy achieved these things. This was not because there was no space but because Marx did not know. However, he immediately set out to fill in the gaps in his understanding by producing *The German Ideology* (1846) in which he tries to explain both how a relatively backward country such as Germany could produce a highly sophisticated theory like Hegelianism, as well as how the particular character of Germany's backwardness explains the theory's mistaken understandings. Of more interest than Marx's explanations of these phenomena in the present context is the simple fact that he develops his theory in a realist manner by developing a model that is then used to explain something.

At the core of his explanation is a simple theoretical model of social life as comprising three elements: productive forces (tools, labour and raw materials), the division of labour, and forms of 'internal intercourse' (ideas, culture, law, and so forth conceptualized as 'ideology') (see Figure 3.2). The interrelationships between these elements, when combined with historical data, are used to account for social and therefore intellectual change and to generate substantive models of the five different types of social formation that Marx understood as marking the successive phases of human social evolution: primitive communism, slavery, feudalism, capitalism, and a hoped for advanced communism. After the *German Ideology* Marx continued to develop his theory and its associated models by applying them to contemporary events in what are commonly referred to as his political writings of the period 1848–62, although it must be acknowledged that this was forced on him by his desperate need for money rather than for self-conciously metatheoretical reasons. Reflecting his need for money, many of these pieces were written for a New York newspaper and were global in scope in that they related to events on three continents – Europe, America and Asia. However, the best known of these political writings today are two that mainly concerned events in Europe, the *Communist Manifesto* (1848) and *The Eighteenth Brumaire of Louis Bonaparte* (1852). In the former, he crystallized his theory and models in a way that he hoped would have popular appeal and in so doing foregrounded his concepts of class and class struggle for the first time. In the latter, which was an analysis of recent political events in France, he focused on the state and its relationships with the other elements that comprise social formations, again for the first time. In sum, then, and in the realist mode, Marx developed his theory by using his model(s) to generate explanations whose insufficiencies required him to produce additional concepts, which then had to be integrated into the theory as a whole.

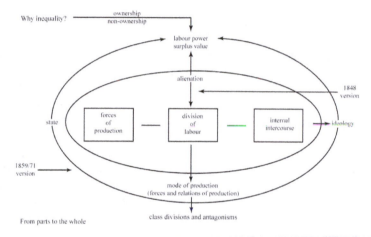

Figure 3.2 Marx, the problem of inequality and the transformation of his theory

Eventually this work of integration required Marx to recast his whole theory. This recasting began with an intensive period of research in the British Museum Library and the production of the associated flood of somewhat fevered and, in his lifetime, unpublished words we know today as the *Grundrisse* (Outline) of 1858. He did, however, publish a short summary of his recast theory under the none-too-alluring title of *A Preface to a Contribution to a Critique of Political Economy* (1859). This includes the famous passage in which Marx outlines almost his whole theory and which is quoted in full below so that you can see what realist social theory looks like – that is, a set of interlinked concepts expressed verbally to produce a model rather than mathematically to represent a law. The passage begins with an outline of Marx's model of society:

the general conclusion at which I arrived and which, once reached, became the guiding principle of my studies, ... can be summarised as follows. In the social production of their life, men enter into definite relations that are indispensable and independent of their will, *relations of production* which correspond to a definite stage of development of their material *productive forces*. The sum total of these relations of production constitutes the *economic structure of society*, the real foundation, on which rises a *legal and political superstructure* and to which correspond definite *forms of social consciousness*. The *mode of production* of material life conditions the social, political and intellectual life process in general. It is not the consciousness of men that determines their being, but, on the contrary, their social being that determines their consciousness.

(Emphasis added to pick out conceptual terms.)

The passage then moves on to apply the model:

At a certain stage of their development, the material productive forces of society come in conflict with the existing relations of production, or – what is but a legal expression for the same thing – with the property relations within which they have been at work hitherto. From forms of development of the productive forces these relations turn into their fetters. Then begins an epoch of social revolution. With the change of the economic foundation the entire immense superstructure is more or less rapidly transformed. In considering such transformations a distinction should always be made between the material transformation of the economic conditions of production, which can be determined with the precision of natural science, and the legal, political, religious, aesthetic or philosophic – in short, ideological forms in which men become conscious of this conflict and fight it out. Just as our opinion of an individual is not based on what he thinks of himself, so can we not judge of such a period of transformation by its own consciousness; on the contrary, this consciousness must be explained rather from the contradictions of material life, from the existing conflict between the social productive forces and the relations of production. No social order ever perishes before all the productive forces for which there is room in it have developed; and new, higher relations of production never appear before the material conditions of their existence have matured in the womb of the old society itself. Therefore mankind always sets itself only such tasks as it can solve; since, looking at the matter more closely, it will always be found that the task itself arises only when the material conditions of its solution already exist or are at least in the process of formation. In broad outlines Asiatic, ancient, feudal, and modern bourgeois modes of production can be designated as progressive epochs in the economic formation of society. The bourgeois relations of production are the last antagonistic form of the social process of production – antagonistic not in the sense of individual antagonisms, but of one arising from the social conditions of life of the individuals; at the same time the productive forces developing in the womb of bourgeois society create the material conditions for the solution of that antagonism. This social formation brings, therefore, the prehistory of society to a close.

The presence of a set of concepts, and the way in which they are used to create a model which is then applied, is self-evident so no further comment is necessary. What may be helpful, however, is a brief account of what the visual effect of reading this passage might be in the case of a contemporary reader:

1   We are immediately invited to think about our own work lives and our lack of control over them, which means that we are already picturing reality as we have experienced it: 'In the social production of their life men enter into definite relations that are indispensible and independent of our will, relations of production ...' – images of ourselves having to get up at a certain time every morning, workplaces, rules and regulations, supervisors and managers, punishments, and wage packets.
2   We are invited to look around and not just see images of factories, laws and lawyers, governments and politicians but see them, metaphorically, as a house wherein the factories are the foundation (base) and the laws etc. are the rooms or floors of the house (superstructure).
3   We are asked to transfer our metaphorical understanding to the historical realm and grasp the fact that sometimes the social superstructure of laws etc. can become too heavy for the foundations represented by productive forces to bear, with the result that they can no longer operate effectively and, like a top-heavy building, the whole social structure begins to wobble and break up as it enters a period of revolutionary turmoil and eventually reconstruction – images of idle factories and striking workers are seen as connected to images of street demonstrations, mass meetings, violence.
4   We are directly asked to picture ourselves in such a period of turmoil and reconstruction and warned that it will be hard to understand what is going on since the spokespeople for the old order will deny everything and we will tend to believe them, unless we remember that it takes time for developments at the foundational level to become apparent at the superstructural

level – images of politicians and spin doctors denying anything significant is going on and talking instead of criminals and terrorists.

5   Finally, we are admonished to have confidence, since history is on the side of the oppressed – unfortunately, today what comes to mind are disturbing images of Stalin, Mao, and George W. Bush, done in the style of Francis Bacon. (http://www.artcyclopedia.com – 'Artist Search')

Of course, this passage, as in the case of Marx's theorizing more generally, is easier to turn into a set of images than that of some other practitioners because the picture of capitalist society projected by his theory has since become part of the culture of many societies, at least where socialist or communist parties have been influential. Also, it should be said that Marx saw himself as a teacher/politician rather than as a philosopher: as he says in the last of his *Theses on Feuerbach*, 'philosophers have only *interpreted* the world in various ways; the point, however, is to change it.' Hence, the personalized way of addressing the reader and the very strong architectural and therefore visual base/superstructure metaphor apparent in the passage reproduced above from his 1859 *Preface*. As will be further illustrated below, Marx almost always makes an effort to help the reader see what he sees even when he is concerned with very abstract concepts pertaining to invisible relationships or processes. This is also what makes Marx a good example to start with in learning how substantive theories function as picturing machines. All theories are picturing machines, but some pictures are much harder to see or make sense of than others. Thus, if Marx because of his realism is the social-theoretical equivalent of J.M.W. Turner (http://www.artcyclopedia.com – 'Artist Search'), who is rather easy to make sense of even when he is making an abstract point, then it seems to me that because of his irrealism Talcott Parsons (see below, pp. 111–15), for example, is the equivalent of an American Expressionist like Mark Rothko (http://www.artcyclopedia.com – 'Artist Search'), who is much harder to fathom unless you already have a trained eye.

Returning to Marx's research strategy and his developing theory, and as has already been shown, by 1859 he had produced his familiar set of concepts – 'mode of production', 'classes', 'class struggle', 'state', and 'ideology' – but he had neither completed them, organized them into a coherent system, nor anywhere near fully developed their implications. All this he set out to do in his next project which resulted in the three published volumes of *Capital*, several large fragments of further volumes, and famously petered out just as he was about to formalize his concept of class. Despite the incomplete realization of his project, Marx fulfilled most of his goals, most importantly completing his system of basic concepts with those of 'labour power' and 'surplus value' and so finally explaining how exploitation is achieved under capitalism see Figure 3.2:

In order to be able to extract value from the consumption of a commodity, our friend, Moneybags [the capitalist], must be so lucky as
to find, within the sphere of circulation, in the market, a commodity whose use-value possesses the peculiar property of being a
source of value, whose actual consumption, therefore, is itself an
embodiment of labour, and, consequently, a creation of value. The
possessor of money does find on the market such a special commodity in capacity for labour or labour-power.

By labour-power or capacity for labour is to be understood the
aggregate of those mental and physical capabilities existing in a
human being, which he exercises whenever he produces a use-
value of any description ...

Accompanied by Mr Moneybags and by the possessor of
labour-power, we therefore take leave for a time of this noisy
sphere, where everything takes place on the surface and in
the view of all men, and follow them into the hidden abode
of production.

(Marx 1965: 176)

Marx's point is that what the capitalist pays the worker is determined
by the cost of maintaining the worker's capacity for work (labour-power),
whilst the capitalist uses that capacity to produce goods that have a higher
value than the worker's wages. The excess value appropriated by the capitalist is what Marx calls 'surplus value' and its continuing extraction from
the worker is deemed to be essential to the continuing health and even survival of capitalism because, in the end, profits depend on it. When I say 'in
the end', I mean it both in the sense that surplus value is what ultimately
makes profits possible and in the sense that it takes Marx the remaining
chapters of the first volume of *Capital* and the two subsequent volumes to
specify the intervening processes and before he can set out what is mis-
leadingly referred to as 'the *law* of the tendency of profit to fall'. The reason
why the term 'law' is misleading in this context is because the substantive
claim concerning profits is not the product of the hypothetico-deductive
loop beloved of the law-seeking logical positivists, but instead the product
of a remarkably detailed generic model of capitalist society. That is, Marx's
'law' is a theoretical deduction from this model rather than a generalization
based on observations and experiments, as is confirmed by the fact that
Marx's seldom-quoted full description of what he had discovered was 'the
law of the tendency of the rate of profit to fall *and its counteracting influences*' (emphasis added) – a law states a necessary relationship whereas what
Marx does is crystallize a set of different possibilities that had been made
apparent by his model (for a concrete application of a developed version of
this model to postwar American society, see Woodiwiss 1993).

In sum, although Marx's metatheory remained largely implicit, it is clear from the character of both the ontological assumptions that he did make explicit and the epistemological assumptions implicit in the research strategy that he pursued in his search for an explanation for inequality, that he was a metatheoretical realist. Indeed he was an exemplary realist in that his strategy: 1) began with the application and critique of existing substantive theory; 2) moved on to modelling social life by combining his emerging new theory with historical and contemporary data; 3) involved the formulation, application and assessment of explanations; and 4) completed its first round, so to speak, by using these assessments to revise and elaborate his initial theory. More generally, his work and some of the uses made of it subsequently are also excellent exemplifications of both the fact that theories are picturing machines and of the sometimes rather frightening social and political power possessed by the images they produce.

Durkheim: seeing things

If the question that provoked Marx's effort to understand the nature of social life was 'why inequality?', the question that provoked Durkheim's effort was 'what is morality?' Notwithstanding their shared preoccupation with the nature of capitalist society and its injustices (Pearce 1989), the difference between these two questions explains not only a lot about the different substantive foci of their two bodies of work, but also a lot about the different ways they went about developing their theories. Marx's question focuses on a particular relationship between two or more parties and answering it required him to work outwards from this relationship so as to uncover the other entities and processes that explain the existence and persistence of the inequality between the two parties – in sum and simplifying somewhat, Marx pictured the parts before he pictured the whole. By contrast, Durkheim's question concerns an attribute of societies as a whole and so led him to begin his theorizing by inquiring into what other equally general entities or processes might explain the existence of morality. Only if he thought the investigation of them might advance his understanding of the social whole, or after he was satisfied that he understood the whole, did Durkheim concern himself with more particular entities and processes – in sum and again simplifying somewhat, Durkheim pictured the whole before he pictured the parts (see Figure 3.3). The following account of Durkheim's research strategy will therefore replicate his priorities by focusing on how he theorized the social whole. Another justification for such an approach is that it enables me to focus on what many people have felt is the hardest aspect of his work to grasp or, as I think they mean, see. This is his conception of social facts as things.

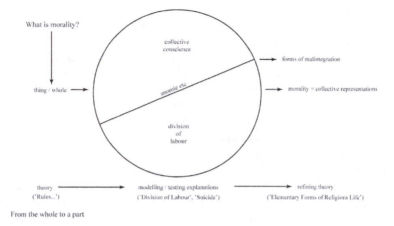

Figure 3.3 Durkheim, the problem of morality and theory construction

As it happens, simply understanding Durkheim to have been a realist, which is common today (Keat and Urry 1975; Benton 1977; Pearce 1989), rather than an empiricist or positivist, removes one of the most common obstacles to seeing what he meant when he urged that social facts should be considered as things. I say this because, depending on the context, Durkheim meant two rather different things by this admonition. The first meaning was that social life should be approached through the study of its visible aspects or appearances as in the case of the natural sciences. Until recently, and often too because Durkheim used the word 'fact', this argument was taken as indicative of his positivism. Actually, all he meant was that social life should be approached scientifically, which at the time, and to repeat, was not a clearly defined idea, except that, as in Comte's case too, it meant more than Humean empiricism and indeed often meant that the study of social life should be approached in a manner that we would now call realist (Hirst 1975). The second meaning was that social life consists of *sui generis* entities and processes and therefore 'represents a specific reality which has its own characteristics' (Durkheim 1988: 129), that 'have *not* as their causes certain states of consciousness of individuals' (Durkheim 1988: 131, emphasis added). Too often the second meaning is forgotten when the first one is rejected.

In any event, and to repeat, the ontological assumptions of empiricism/positivism and realism are the same and, as the two meanings Durkheim gave to the idea of treating social facts as things indicate, he was committed to the views that society existed independently of human minds and was accessible through our senses, notably our sense of sight. This said, there remains a tension between the two meanings because insisting that sociology should be constructed on the basis of the study of what is visible would seem to indicate an empiricist epistemology and rule out the possibility of social facts being *sui generis* things, because no one has ever seen such things as those Durkheim spoke about, as in the cases of the 'conscience collective', the 'division of labour', 'anomie', 'suicidogenic cur-rents', or 'collective representations'. Durkheim may not have been aware of such a tension, nor indeed of the theoretically rather than empirically derived character of his social things. However, he was certainly and explic-itly aware of at least the initial invisibility of 'social things' to most people and he therefore went to great lengths to help them see what he saw. In so doing, he adopted, consciously or otherwise, what we would now call a realist epistemology and research strategy. Thus, as will be shown below, his programme of work began with the critical adoption of existing substantive theory, proceeded to substantive modeling, the derivation of explanations, and the assessment of their adequacy, before ending with the refinement and elaboration of the initial theory. Moreover, a lot of his theorizing of particular institutions and processes was also the by-product of his effort to make the more general entities and processes visible to others, as will also be shown below.

This is how Durkheim introduced the idea of social things in his first lecture as a university teacher in 1887:

> Since Plato and his Republic, there has been no lack of thinkers who have philosophized about the nature of societies. But until the beginning of this century, most of this work was dominated by an idea which radically prevented the establishment of sociology. In effect, nearly all these political theorists saw society as a human creation, a product of art and reflection. According to them, men began to live together because they found that it was useful and good: society is an invention which they thought up in order to better their condition a little. According to this view, a nation is not a natural product, like organisms or plants, which are born, which grow and develop through some internal necessity. Rather, it resembles the machines which men make by assembling parts according to a preconceived plan. If the cells of an adult animal's body become what they are, it is because it was in their nature to become that. If they are aggregated in a specific way, it is because, given the existing milieu, it was impossible for them to be aggre-gated in any other ... Well, shouldn't it be the same way with society ... ?
>
> (Traugott 1978: 44–5)

Clearly, Durkheim knew he was saying something very radical so he must have been very confident, given that this was after all his first lecture as a university teacher. His confidence stemmed from the work he had already done in connection with his doctoral dissertation which was published six years later in 1893 as *The Division of Labour*. He was also from the beginning a very astute intellectual publicist, since despite the fact that the theories he was actually responding to were those of Comte, Toennies and Spencer (Lukes 1973: 140–7), he appears to have realized that, if he wanted his ideas to stand a chance of making even an academic, let alone a wider, impact, he had to relate them to more general and popular ideas and debates, if possible by presenting his own ideas as both a radical critique of, and alternative to, such ideas. Thus, although Durkheim's fundamental point concerning the existence of social things could have been made in many other ways and he was not in fact responding to Marxist ideas as such, he chose to present his 'big idea' by calling into question the economic determinism of the then highly influential socialist movement. And he decided to do this in what appears to have been an intentionally provocative way; that is, by demonstrating that morality, which the socialists considered a hopelessly sentimental, old-fashioned and even reactionary idea, was also important in determining the course and consequences not just of social development in general but of the development of the economy in particular. Both the strategic and provocative aspects of his intervention therefore may be seen to have been reflected in his choice or acceptance of the title, *The Division of Labour*, for his book in that it would attract socialist readers who would then be scandalized by its content and, he hoped, forced to react to it.

The Division of Labour, then, represents the beginning of what turned out to be a lifelong effort to make visible the existence of social facts in general and morality in particular. Thus early on in the book, and after identifying social facts in general as responsible for the sense of external constraint people experience in many areas of their lives, and morality in particular, with a variety of such constraint derived from what he termed social solidarity, Durkheim acknowledges that the problem is that such solidarity is not something that is directly visible. However, he immediately suggests that there is a set of institutions that can serve as a 'visible index' of social solidarity and its changing character, namely the set relating to the law. Moreover, 'since law reproduces the principal forms of social solidarity, we have only to classify the different types of law to find therefrom the different types of social solidarity which correspond to it (sic)' (Durkheim 1997a: 68). In his view legal rules may be best classified for sociological purposes on the basis of 'the different sanctions which are attached to them' (Durkheim 1997a: 69) which results in the differentiation of 'two great classes' of legal rules, those that have repressive sanctions attached to them and those that have restitutive sanctions attached to them: 'the first comprises all penal [criminal] law; the second, civil law, commercial law, procedural law, administrative and constitutional law ...' (Durkheim 1997a: 69). Reasoning back from these two types of law, he posits two different modes of social solidarity. First, because penal law originates in social conditions marked by a very low level of the division of labour (as in the case of tribal societies), wherein there are, for example, no markets, social cohesion can only be maintained by the rigorous enforcement of a shared morality that he terms the 'conscience collective'. He calls the mode of solidarity characteristic of such societies 'mechanical solidarity'. Second, because restitutive law emerges and develops as the division of labour becomes more complex and markets, for example, proliferate, social cohesion is increasingly maintained spontaneously by the interdependence so produced rather than by the rigorous enforcement of the conscience collective. He calls the mode of solidarity to which restitutive law corresponds, 'organic solidarity'.[1]

Thanks to the empirical detail that Durkheim supplies in the course of these two derivations, two social facts, in the sense of two sources of constraints on individual behaviour, are quickly made visible: 'the division of labour' and the 'conscience collective'. Moreover, he also provides a first glimpse of the thing that is morality, in the form of this definition of the 'conscience collective':

> The totality of beliefs and sentiments common to average citizens of the same society forms a determinate system which has its own life; one may call it the collective or common conscience. No doubt, it has not a specific organ as a substratum; it is, by definition, diffuse in every reach of society. Nevertheless, it has specific characteristics which make it a distinct reality. It is, in effect, independent of the particular conditions in which individuals are placed; they pass on and it remains. It is the same in the North and in the South, in great cities and in small, in different professions. Moreover, it does not change with each generation, but, on the contrary, it connects successive generations with one another. It is, thus, an entirely different thing from particular consciences, although it can be realized only through them. It is the psychical type of society, a type which has its properties, its conditions of existence, its mode of development, just as individual types, although in a different way. Thus understood, it has the right to be denoted by a special word.
>
> (Durkheim 1997: 79–80)

Additionally, in the course of Durkheim's account of the gradual displacement over time of mechanical by organic solidarity as the predominant source of moral and social regulation, pictures are also provided of how such regulation was, first, sacrilized and later secularized or, so to speak, brought back down to earth, as well as of morality's independent determin-ative power. This is how he describes the rise (literally) of religion:

In the beginning, the gods are not distinct from the universe, or rather there are no gods, but only sacred beings, without their sacred character being related to any external entity as their source. The animals or plants of the species which serves as a clan-totem are the objects of worship ... are divine in and of themselves. But little by little religious forces are detached from the things of which they were first only the attributes, and become hypostatized. Thus is formed the notion of spirits or gods who, while residing here or there as preferred, nevertheless exist outside of the particular objects to which they are more specifically attached. By that very fact they are less concrete ... The Graeco–Latin polytheism, which is a more elevated and better organized form of animism, marks new progress in the direction of transcendence ... Set upon the mysterious heights of Olympus or dwelling in the recesses of the earth, they personally intervene in human affairs only in some-what intermittent fashion. But it is only with Christianity that God takes leave of space; his kingdom is no longer of this world ... The God of humanity necessarily is less concrete than the gods of the city or the clan.

(Durkheim 1997: 288–9)

And this is how, anticipating insights generated by Foucault's concept of 'governmentality' by 80 or so years (see below, pp. 146–7), Durkheim describes morality's return to earth in the writings of such early political economists as Adam Smith and as exemplified by the appearance of the idea of liberty that became central to the ethic of market societies:

They have, however, been mistaken as to the nature of this liberty. Since they see it as a constitutive attribute of man, since they log-ically deduce it from the concept of the individual in itself, it seems to them to be entirely a state of nature, leaving aside all of society. Social action, according to them, has nothing to add to it; all that it can and must do is to regulate the external functioning in such a way that the competing liberties do not harm one another. And, if it is not strictly confined within these limits, it encroaches on the legitimate domain of the individual and diminishes it. But, besides the fact that it is false to believe that all regulation is the product of constraint, it happens that liberty itself is the product of regula-tion. Far from being antagonistic to social action, it results from social action. It is far from being an inherent property of the state of nature. On the contrary, it is a conquest of society over nature.

(Durkheim 1997a: 386–7)

In sum, Durkheim made remarkable progress towards his goal of making social facts, and morality in particular, visible to others in the course of his first book – no wonder he was so confident in that first lecture. But a new way of seeing is seldom established by a single demonstration given the resistances it encounters, especially from those committed to different metatheories and/or other theories. Besides, despite his progress, Durkheim probably knew that the real prizes still eluded him, namely understandings of what morality in itself consisted of and how exactly it achieves its effects.

For these reasons, then, and with the huge benefit of hindsight, one can read the next stages in his unfolding research programme as a process of gearing himself up to make the final assault on these twin peaks. In *The Rules of Sociological Method* of 1895, he may be read as checking his metatheoretical and methodological equipment (Woodiwiss 2001: 47–56). In *Suicide* of 1897 he may be read as testing this equipment again by using it to try finally to convince his readers of the reality and power of social facts and their interrelationships by demonstrating their pertinence to even the most private and desperate of individual acts. And in his research and writings concerning 'primitive' religions and especially their sacrificial practices he may be read as establishing his base camp.

The record of the climb that followed is contained in *The Elementary Forms of Religious Life* of 1912. The high points were the specification of morality's substance, so to speak, made possible by his concept of 'collective representations', and the account of how exactly religion and, by extension, morality achieves its effects on individuals. 'Collective representations' are defined by contrasting and connecting them with 'individual representations'. Thus, whereas the latter refer to the particular ideas that individuals carry around in their heads, the former refer to the general ideas that the members of a specific society share and which both derive from, and regulate, their collective life by giving content to and organizing the structure of individual representational systems. Examples of collective representations include the ideas of time and space, as well as myriad classification systems concerning everything from plants, through animals to people (Durkheim 1995: 10–11).

The much more substantive understanding of the nature of the *conscience collective* that resulted is presented as follows:

> In order that the [*conscience collective*] may appear, a synthesis *sui generis* of particular consciousnesses is required. Now this synthesis has the effect of disengaging a whole world of sentiments, ideas and images which once born, obey laws all their own. They attract each other, repel each other, unite, divide themselves, and multiply, though these combinations are not commanded and necessitated by the condition of the underlying reality. The life thus

brought into being even enjoys so great an independence that it sometimes indulges in manifestations with no purpose or utility of any sort, for the mere pleasure of affirming itself We have shown that this is often precisely the case with ritual activity and mythological thought.

(Durkheim 1995: 423–4)

And finally, this is his account of how morality achieves its effects:

An individual or collective subject is said to inspire respect when the representation that expresses it in consciousness has such power that it calls forth or inhibits conduct automatically irrespective of any utilitarian calculation of helpful or harmful results. When we obey someone out of respect for the moral authority that we have accorded to him, we do not follow his instructions because they seem wise but because a certain psychic energy intrinsic to the idea we have of that person bends our will and turns it in the direction indicated. When that inward and wholly mental pressure moves within us, respect is the emotion we feel. We are then moved not by the advantages or disadvantages of the conduct that is recommended to us or demanded of us but by the way we conceive of the one who recommends or demands that conduct. This is why a command generally takes on short, sharp forms of address that leave no room for hesitation. It is also why, to the extent that command is command and works by its own strength, it precludes any idea of deliberation or calculation, but instead is made effective by the very intensity of the mental state in which it is given. That intensity is what we call moral influence.

(Durkheim 1995: 423–4)

Like Marx, Durkheim does not simply describe what can be seen but, in a realist manner, he shows us how abstract concepts can enable us to see familiar things differently both by producing new data and by modelling the presentation of the data in ways that alter our perception of social life. Borrowing from biology, the summary image of the social that Durkheim produced pictured it as a series of life forms distinguished by: first, their distinctive, externally visible 'morphological' shapes or the bounded forms produced by the interactions between the division of labour and the sphere of representations; and second, their consequently equally distinctive interior 'physiologies' or the institutional structures whereby and wherein the detailed binding together of the morphological elements occurs (Traugott 1978: 71–90). Figure 3.3 summarizes this image and the research strategy that produced it.

Again like Marx, Durkheim died before he could fully answer the question that had initiated his quest in the sense that he only managed to write the introduction to what was to be the book about morality, *La Morale*. Thus, in the same way that Marx's legacy to sociology included not just the more or less finished elements of his theory but also the spur to theoretical and investigatory creativity represented by the unfinished elements, especially those relating to class, then Durkheim's legacy also included both finished and unfinished elements that have continued to define the discipline's research agenda as well as its theoretical core. In Durkheim's case, it is particularly his concern with theorizing the nature of cultural phenomena that has continued to dominate the agenda, most notably in the form of Foucault's work (see below, pp. 101–3), whilst most recently his concern with morality has also resurfaced as a sociological interest in human rights has gradually emerged (Woodiwiss 2005, Chapter 11).

Notes

1   It is important to note that, contrary to what is said in many introductory texts and many others whose authors ought to know better, Durkheim did not argue that there was an historical movement from retributive to restitutive law but that there was an historical movement whereby retributive penal law was *augmented* by restitutive civil law as the division of labour became more elaborate and the basis of social solidarity changed; that is, penal law remained retributive but was joined by civil law that was restitutive.

4   Looking from the inside

One of the surprising things about sociology's foundational period from our globalized vantage point is how little the classical theorists knew about each other's work. Of course, Marx (1818–83) had died before Durkheim (1858–1917) and Weber (1864–1920) had published anything of note, and both of them knew of Marx's ideas even if they do not appear to have been serious students of his work. But neither Durkheim nor Weber had much knowledge of each other's work despite their prominence in their home countries. This said, had Weber, at least as represented in the typical introductory textbook, encountered Durkheim's claims that social phenomena should be understood and treated as things, he would most likely have used them as an implausibly extreme example of everything that he defined his own position against. In return, but again only in response to the textbook stereotype, Durkheim would have regarded Weber as like ' all the ... political theorists [who] saw society as a human creation' (see above, p. 48) and therefore as an obstacle to sociology's establishment. One of the prime exhibits Durkheim could have presented would have been Weber's apparently very individualistic definition of sociology:

> Sociology ... is a science which attempts the interpretive understanding of social action in order thereby to arrive at a causal explanation of its course and effects. In 'action' is included all human behaviour when and insofar as the acting individual attaches a subjective meaning to it.
>
> (Weber 1947a: 88–9)

Another, again apparently, would have been this compounding of the error:

> For ... other cognitive purposes – for instance, juristic ones – or for practical ends, it may ... be convenient or even indispensable to treat social collectivities, such as states, associations, business corporations, foundations, as if they were individual persons ... But

for the subjective interpretation of action in sociological work these collectivities must be treated as *solely* the resultants and modes of organization of the particular acts of individual persons since these alone can be treated as agents in a course of subjectively understandable action.

(Weber ibid: 101–2)

In sum, then, and on the basis of such evidence, Weber is commonly understood to have been Durkheim's theoretical opposite. Thus the pictures of social life that their theories project are also commonly thought to be very different. In Durkheim's case the reader struggles to try to see the things rather than people that he tells us are there; whereas in Weber's case, one rather too easily tends to see a picture of individuals and groups pursuing their ends, conversing, interacting rather than the structural things he is in fact most often trying to bring to our attention. Regrettably, but only because it complicates the expository enterprise, this would seem to be a very exaggerated contrast for reasons that will be given below. However, it must first be acknowleged that there are grounds upon which this contrast could be justified. These derive from the undeniable fact that they were each formally committed to very different sets of metatheoretical assumptions. As was argued in the previous chapter, Durkheim was a realist, whereas Weber regarded himself as what I am terming an interpretivist, indeed Weber more or less invented the combination of an idealist ontology with an empiricist epistemology that interpretivism represents. On this basis you might expect that the two theorists would produce very different pictures of social life. In fact there is no such radical difference because Weber did not allow his ontological idealism to have much of an effect on his research practice, despite it being the most striking element of his metatheory, (Woodiwiss 2001: Chapter 1).

The question therefore arises as to why Weber chose to claim that he based his effort to picture social life on an idealist ontology that his peers, known and unknown, were so strongly convinced was not simply mistaken but also historically anachronistic. The three reasons that will have to serve as the answer in the present instance may be summarized as follows: neo-Kantianism, hermeneutics and George Simmel. Today, Immanuel Kant (1724–1804) is universally regarded as one of the most important philosophers of all time. One of the reasons for this reputation is that, reacting to Hume, Kant synthesized the leading ideas of the empiricist and rationalist traditions by arguing that reason and vision had to be combined in the pursuit of knowledge – reason makes knowledge possible by organizing perception but only vision can provide content. For Kant, this meant that scientific knowledge was limited to those aspects of things we can see – phenomena (appearances) – and did not extend to the invisible inner structure of things – the noumena (things in themselves). This argument was both a breakthrough and a challenge to later philosophers in that many of them tried to use the positive first part of it to refute the limitations imposed by the second part. Thus Kant's argument both made possible Hegel's idealism and its diverse progeny, and it could also have given some philosophical legitimacy to the ordinary realism that appears to have informed the activities of practising scientists during the nineteenth century, had the scientists sought it.

Despite or because of his significance, Kant's own position was neglected for a while until interest in it was revived in the 1860s and in the form of neo-Kantianism. Neo-Kantianism represented yet another attempt to use Kant to surpass Kant; in other words, its adherents argued that, whereas Kant was correct in arguing that the possibility of knowledge of the natural world was limited to its phenomenal side, Kant was not correct as regards knowledge of human cultural life, because its inner, noumenal side too was in fact accessible if not exactly visible to us because, as human beings, we are always already within it. And what made such access possible was a technique invented by the German theologian Friedrich Schliermacher (1768–1834) which became known as hermeneutics or empathetic interpretation. Hermeneutics, which is only possible because of a shared humanity, involves reconstructing the thought of another in your own mind so that you can clarify its meaning. Finally, it was Simmel, of course an important sociologist in his own right, who convinced Weber that, while hermeneutics should be the predominant approach to the study of social life, there was also a role for an observation-based and therefore more science-like approach in verifying interpretations.

These, then, were the ideas that Weber combined with his own underlying Kantian more than neo-Kantian insistence that the study of social phenomena should be approached scientifically in that it should involve the articulation of reason with careful observation. For this reason, it seems to me that the best way of looking at Weber's conception of the research process is to see it as a complication of the empiricist conception (see Figure 4.1). The critical difference between Figure 4.1 and Figure 2.1 is that, although the separate squares in the background that represent mind and matter are repeated in order to indicate Weber's underlying empiricism, they are presented as overlapping. This is to suggest the reduction of the gap between mind and matter that is a consequence of Weber's acceptance of the idealist ontological assumptions of the neo-Kantians as regards our internal vantage point with respect to the cultural realm. Thus, almost by definition, the ideas that populate much of the cultural realm depend on people thinking of them for their existence; ideas as such are immaterial and so not directly accessible through the senses; and, because the producers/carriers of ideas are individual human beings, it is they rather than any *sui generis* social thing, that should be the focus of attention. Although again the flow diagram in the foreground is the same as that in Figure 2.1, the difference made by its articulation with an idealist rather than an empiricist ontology is indicated by the use of Weber's methodological vocabulary in place of that of the empiricists.

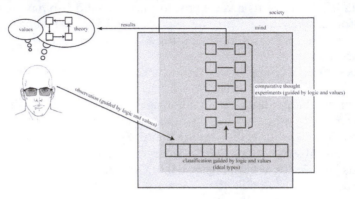

Figure 4.1 Weber, the problem of observation and theory construction (formal position)

Put into words, the critical consequence for the research process of Weber's ontological commitment to the idea that social life is primarily a matter of ideas or meanings is that, since the latter are an 'absolute infinity' (Weber 1949: 82), some basis for selecting the meanings to be investigated has to be found. Weber suggests that this basis should be the values and interests of the investigator, provided, and this point is most often neglected in the textbooks, that they *'have the necessary "point of view" ... [in that] they must understand how to relate the events of the real world consciously or unconsciously to universal "cultural values"'* (Weber 1949: 81–2, emphasis added). This is for two reasons: first, selection according to relevence to value happens anyway and is therefore both legitimated by, and consistent with, the neo-Kantian claim that we are always already inside culture; secondly and consequently, selection on the basis of universal values ensures that the research effort is devoted to culturally significant rather than trivial matters. Moreover, and again contrary to much of what is said in introductory textbooks, it is important to realize that the relevance of values does not end with the selection of the research topic but extends to the processes of observation and classification, as well as those of hypothesis formulation and testing.

Picturing rationality

Although observation is given its point, so to speak, by being primarily concerned to elucidate the meanings of the relevant actors and is therefore

described as a process of *verstehen* or empathetic understanding, the investigator's 'own' values also, indeed must, play a significant role in determining what are presented as the actors' values. This is because:

> In the great majority of cases actual action goes on in a state of
> inarticulate half-consciousness or actual unconsciousness of its
> subjective meaning ... The ideal type of meaningful action where
> the meaning is fully conscious and explicit is the marginal case.
> Every sociological or historical investigation, in applying its analy-
> sis to the empirical facts must take this fact into account ...
> [Nevertheless] [h]e may reason as if action actually proceeded on
> the basis of clearly self-conscious meaning.
>
> (Weber 1949: 22)

For this reason, and with the exception of his famous study of the
'Protestant ethic' (Weber 1904), Weber does not present the results of his
observations in the form of detailed textual commentaries or enthnogra-
phies that provide very detailed pictures of small corners of the social
world, as would most likely be the case today if one were claiming to be representing the meanings of others. Instead, these meanings are most often
presented in the summary, abstract and general form represented by his
'ideal types' . The latter were so named for the following reason:

> An ideal type is formed by the one-sided accentuation of one or
> more points of view and by the synthesis of a great many diffuse,
> discrete, more or less present and occasionally absent concrete indi-
> vidual phenomena, which are arranged according to those one-
> sidedly emphasized viewpoints into a unified analytical construct.
>
> (Weber 1949: 90)

Parsons, very influentially, referred to the type of picturing of social life
that resulted from this mode of research as 'mosaical' (Parsons 1937: 607).
His point was that it consisted of a loosely integrated or not clearly pat-
terned set of economic, political and cultural relationships, institutions and
entities such as classes and status groups which, Parsons suggests, Weber
would be happy to concede might well be composed differently if the work
involved were to be repeated by someone else.

However, after rereading Weber's major works once again in preparing
for the present project, I am no longer as sure as I was in the past that this
is in fact the sort of image of society that Weber sought to project. For, if
Weber's rather snooty dismissal of people's capacity for self-awareness and
his preference for points of view rooted in 'universal cultural values' were
two reasons for his resort to ideal types, a third, and it seems to me more
important reason, and indeed one which makes a deeper sense of the first

two, was that his primary concern was with the construction of explanations. And this, in turn, was because he regarded such activity as unfortunately as close as sociology can ever come to the formulation of 'laws'
because of the difficulties intrinsic to the process of verificaction in the
social domain:

> Unfortunately this type of verification is feasible with relative accu-
> racy only in the few very special cases susceptible of psychological
> experimentation. The approach to a satisfactory degree of accuracy
> is exceedingly various, even in the limited number of cases of mass
> phenomena which can be statistically described and unambigu-
> ously interpreted. For the rest there remains only the possibility of
> comparing the largest possible number of historical or contempo-
> rary processes which, while otherwise similar, differ in the one
> decisive point of their relation to the particular motive or factor
> the role of which is being investigated. This is a fundamental task
> of comparative sociology. Often, unfortunately, there is available
> only the dangerous and uncertain procedure of the 'imaginary
> experiment' which consists in thinking away certain elements of a
> chain of motivation and working out the course of action which
> would then probably ensue, thus arriving at a causal judgment.
>
> (Weber 1947a: 97)

Thus, although Weber considered the establishment of social laws to be
highly improbable, and notwithstanding his formal adoption of certain
neo-Kantian positions, he was equally clear that sociologists should act as
if the establishment of laws was possible and conduct their research in
accordance with natural science protocols. This, then, may be the reason he
set such an undemanding standard with regard to establishing what he
termed the 'adequacy at the level of meaning' of any interpretation. This
standard was that 'according to our habitual modes of thought and feeling,
its component parts taken in their mutual relation are recognized to constitute a '"typical" complex of meaning' (Weber 1947a: 99). It may also
have been the source of his commitment to 'universal cultural values' as
providing the basis for the non-trivial interpretation of the meaning of
social action, because such values also provided him with a supposedly
general vantage point and so reduced the danger that his reasoning powers
would be unnecessarily constrained by having to reconcile too many details
with any explanation he wished to make. Finally, it perhaps also explains
why, as his thought developed, Weber became much more concerned with
'causal adequacy' than with 'meaning adequacy'. And in a way that,
notwithstanding his formal epistemological commitments, suggests his
adherence to a realist rather than an empiricist conception of social-scientific practice (this point is justified at some length in Woodiwiss 2001:

Chapter 1). Consequently, Weber's major theoretical text, *Economy and Society*, summarizes his life's work, or so it appears to me, by constructing a series of varyingly elaborated social models around his four ideal types of action: *Zweckrationale* (purposively rational) action where both the ends and means of action are concrete with the result that it is possible to calculate the degree of success or failure, as in the case of profit – the predominant form of action under capitalism; *wertrationale* (value-rational) action where the means are concrete but not the ends so that, although the means may be manipulated, the degree of one's sucesss in achieving one's goals is not knowable, as in the case of salvation – the predominant form of action where societies are in transition from feudalism to capitalism; *traditional* action where both ends and means are adopted because it has ever been thus in the community concerned – the predominant form of action in feudal societies; and *affectual* action where both ends and means are chosen on emotional grounds – the predominant form of action in 'simple societies'.

More particularly his model of capitalism is constructed on the basis of the predominance of *zweckrationale* action:

> that is, [action] determined by expectations as to the behavior of objects in the environment and of other human beings; these expectations are used as 'conditions' or 'means' for the attainment of the actor's own rationally pursued and calculated ends.
>
> (Weber 1968b: 24)

This is what the predominance of *zweckrationale* action means rationality looks like governmentally:

> ... the fundamental categories of rational legal authority [are]:
> (1) A continuous rule-bound conduct of official business.
> (2) A specified sphere of competence (jurisdiction). This involves (a) a sphere of obligations to perform functions which has been marked off as part of a systematic division of labour. (b) The provision of the incumbent with the necessary powers. (c) That the necessary means of compulsion are clearly defined and their use is subject to definite conditions.
>
> (Weber 1968b: 218)

This is what the predominance of *zweckrationale* action means that rationality looks like organizationally:

> The purest type of exercise of legal authority is that which employs a bureaucratic administrative staff. Only the supreme chief of the organization occupies his position of dominance by virtue of

appropriation, of election, or of having been designated for the succession. But even his authority consists in a sphere of legal 'competence'. The whole administrative staff under the supreme authority then consists, in the purest type, of individual officials ... who are appointed and function according to the following criteria:

1 They are personally free and subject to authority only with respect to their impersonal official obligations.

2 They are organized in a clearly defined hierarchy of offices.

3 Each official has a clearly defined sphere of competence in the legal sense.

4 The office is filled by a free contractual relationship. Thus, in principle, there is free selection.

5 Candidates are selected on the basis of technical qualifications. In the most rational case, this is tested by examination or guaranteed by diplomas certifying technical training, or both. They are appointed not elected.

6 They are remunerated by fixed salaries in money, for the most part with a right to pensions. Only under certain circumstances does the employing authority, especially in private organizations, have a right to terminate the appointment, but the official is always free to resign. The salary scale is primarily graded according to rank in the hierarchy; but in addition to this criterion, the responsibility of the position and the requirements of the incumbent's social status may be taken into account.

7 The office is treated as the sole, or at least the primary, occupation of the incumbent.

8 It constitutes a career. There is a system of 'promotion' according to seniority or to achievement, or both. Promotion is dependent on the judgment of superiors.

9 The official works entirely separated from ownership of the means of administration and without appropriation of his position.

10 He is subject to strict and systematic discipline and control in the conduct of the office.

(Weber 1968b: 220–1)

This is what the predominance of *zweckrationale* action means rationality looks like economically:

The 'capitalistic' orientation of profit-making (in the case of rationality, this means: orientation to capital accounting) can take a number of qualitatively different forms, each of which represents a different type:

1 It may be orientation to profit possibilities in continuous buying
and selling on the market ('trade') with free exchange – that is,
absence of formal and at least relative absence of substantive
compulsion to affect any given exchange; or it may be orientation to the profit possibilities in continuous production of goods
in enterprises with capital accounting.

...

6 It may be orientation to profit opportunities of the following
types: (a) in purely speculative transactions in standardized commodities or in the securities of an enterprise; (b) in the execution
of the continuous financial operations of political bodies; (c) in
the promotional financing of new enterprises in the form of sale
of securities to investors; (d) in the speculative financing of capitalistic enterprises and of various other types of economic
organization with the purpose of a profitable regulation of
market situations or of attaining power

Types (1) and (6) are to a large extent peculiar to the modern
Western World. Other types have been common all over the world
for thousands of years where the possibilities of exchange, money
economy, and money financing have been present.

(Weber 1968b: 164)

Finally, in a pleasant surprise, this is what the predominance of *zweckrationale* action means rationality looks like in the bedroom:

The last accentuation of the erotical sphere occurred in terms of
intellectualist cultures. It occurred where this sphere collided with
the unavoidably ascetic trait of the vocational specialist type of
man. Under this tension between the erotic sphere and rational
everyday life, specifically extramarital sexual life, which had been
removed from everyday affairs, could appear as the only tie which
still linked man with the natural fountain of all life. For man had
now been completely emancipated from the cycle of the old,
simple, and organic existence of the peasant.
   A tremendous value emphasis on the specific sensation of an
inner-worldly salvation from rationalization thus resulted. A
joyous triumph over rationality corresponded in its radicalism
with the unavoidable and equally radical rejection of an ethics of
any kind of other- or supra-worldly salvation. For such ethics, the
triumph of the spirit over the body should find its climax precisely
here, and sexual life could even gain the character of the only and

the ineradicable connection with animality. But this tension between an inner-worldly and an other-worldly salvation from rationality must be sharpest and most unavoidable precisely where the sexual sphere is systematically prepared for a highly valued erotic sensation. This sensation reinterprets and glorifies all the pure animality of the relation, whereas the religion of salvation assumes the character of a religion of love, brotherhood, and neighborly.

Under these conditions, the erotic relation seems to offer the unsurpassable peak of the fulfillment of the request for love in the direct fusion of the souls of one to the other.

(Gerth and Mills 1948: 346–7)

I could go on, but what has already been said indicates that, in making rationality visible as a set of social practices that are repeated across the whole range of social relations, what is produced is a quite elaborate model of capitalist society rather than a mosaic or a series of snapshots taken from different angles. A model that, so far from portraying capitalism as loosely integrated, in fact portrays it as, if anything, oppressively over-integrated. The result is that, again, so far from Weber regarding this picture as merely the projection of a melancholy bourgeois which would not be repeated by someone of a lighter disposition, he considers it in the light of 'universal cultural values' to warrant being described as an 'iron cage' (Weber 1904: 181) whose further development promises only a 'polar night of icy cold and darkness' for everyone (Gerth and Mills 1948: 128).

In the end, then, and in terms of both their modes of theorizing and the nature of the pictures of capitalist society they produced, not just Marx and Durkheim but Weber too may be seen to have had more in common with one another than has usually been imagined. Thus Weber's actual research strategy may be better represented by Figure 5.1 (see below, p. 93) than by Figure 4.1. However, it must be said that a much more widespread conception of what they had in common is the diametrically opposed one set out by Talcott Parsons in his *Structure of Social Action* (1937). This presented the founders, and especially Durkheim and Weber, as converging on what Parsons called the 'voluntaristic theory of action'. The latter has been most often understood as having been largely inspired by the humanistic, neo-Kantian side of Weber only to have been subverted later by the supposedly conservative, functionalist side of Durkheim, as Parsons himself became a functionalist. Why Parsons should have seen the major contributions made by Durkheim and Weber and the relationship between them in this way is something that will be investigated in Part 2. It is mentioned here only because it partially explains why it was that when Weber's work returned to sociological favour in the 1960s, it was as the interpretivist, action-oriented antidote to all-system or structurally-focused sociologies;

that is, he was presented as the proponent of *verstehen* as a self-sufficient methodology in its own right that therefore rendered unnecessary, if it was noticed at all, the empiricist apparatus that Weber, as a man of his scientistic time, maintained in the background.

The Weber whose research strategy is summarized in Figure 4.1 has nevertheless also had his supporters, particularly in Britain and they have happily embraced his empiricist side (see, for example, Lockwood 1958; Goldthorpe, J. *et al.* 1969; Newby 1977 and Marshall *et al.* 1989). However, a far more popular reading of the significance of Weber's work, one that would very definitely have provoked Durkheim's wrath, and which, when required, provided metatheoretical support for the efflorescence of ethnographic studies that occurred during the 1980s, was that provided by Peter Winch (1958). For Winch, Weber's empiricist side was a metaphysical chrysalis that had to be shed if *verstehende soziologie* was finally to fly.

Winch: discoursing the real

The title of Winch's book, *The Idea of a Social Science*, plays nicely with two meanings of the word 'idea': the first is that of a proposed plan as in phrases such as 'I have an idea for a course, party, holiday or whatever'; and the second is the idealist ontological assumption as to the mentalistic or ideational character of social life. In other words, Winch's title announces that the book represents an effort to refound social science and especially sociology on a consistently idealist or rationalist basis. It was, and is, not the only such effort – see, for example, the work of phenomenologists like Alfred Schutz, as well as that of symbolic interactionists, ethnomethodologists, conversational analysts, and 'science, technology, society' writers like Steve Woolgar and Bruno Latour. However, Winch's argument makes essentially the same points as these other social constructionists but without throwing either so much or so little philosophical weight about and consequently more elegantly and concisely. For this reason it will be taken as exemplifying the revival of rationalist thinking in postwar sociology. Winch's strategy is, first, to criticize Weber for his metatheoretical inconsistency in combining an idealist ontology with an empiricist epistemology, and, second, to argue that the former made the latter unnecessary in the case of the social sciences, because once it is accepted that we are inside what we study, gaining knowledge of social life is unproblematic and we simply have to report what people say about it to understand it. Winch's research strategy is as alluringly simple as the rationale behind it is intellectually demanding (see Figure 4.2).

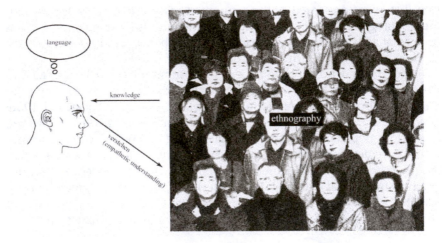

Figure 4.2 Winch, the demystification of language and the irrelevance of theory

Thus, because there is only one ontological dimension (mind is society) rather than two, not only is Weber's insistence on the checking of 'insider' knowledge against the evidence represented by external appearances unnecessary, but so too and very much contrary to much of the rest of the rationalist tradition, is theory. This is because both are only needed if there is a difference, gap or gulf between the researcher and his or her object of study. Here, then, are the reasons why, as with the other approaches I consider his to represent, Winch's 'ideas' became so strongly associated with the ethnographic method or participant observation (seeking to understand social situations by immersing one's self within them): first, the term 'participant' indicates that what is being practised is not external but internal observation; and second, the result of such observation is a record of the discourse of the actors involved which, for Winch and again for those his work represents, is what might be termed 'the stuff' of social life (Winch 1958:128–9).

Since the nature of the discursive stuff that is considered to constitute social life is readily apparent from the talk recorded in any ethnographic study or indeed from the chatter of the daily life of even a moderately gregarious person, it seems unnecessary to give any concrete examples here. Rather, because many readers are likely to consider this very possibility as indicating the preposterous nature of Winch's ideas, the remainder of this section will be devoted to outlining his rationale. This begins with a recounting of a standard realist 'proof' of the existence of the external world and a response to it:

The whole issue was symbolically dramatized on a celebrated occasion in 1939 when Professor G.E. Moore gave a lecture to the

British Academy entitled 'Proof of an External World'. Moore's 'proof' ran roughly as follows. He held up each of his hands in succession, saying 'Here is one hand and here is another; therefore at least two external objects exist; therefore an external world exists'. In arguing thus Moore seemed to be treating the question 'Does an external world exist?' as similar in form to the question 'Do animals with a single horn growing out of their snout exist?' This of course would be conclusively settled by the production of two rhinoceri. But the bearing of Moore's argument on the philosophical question of the existence of an external world is not as simple as the bearing of the production of two rhinoceri on the other question. For, of course, philosophical doubt about the existence of an external world covers the two hands which Moore produced in the same way as it covers everything else. The whole question is: Do objects like Moore's two hands qualify as inhabitants of an external world? This is not to say that Moore's argument is completely beside the point; what is wrong is to regard it as an experimental 'proof', for it is not like anything one finds in an experimental discipline. Moore was not making an experiment; he was reminding his audience of something, reminding them of the way in which the expression 'extenal object' is in fact used. And his reminder indicated that the issue in philosophy is not to prove or disprove the existence of a world of external objects but rather to elucidate the concept of externality. That there is a connection between this issue and the central philosophical problem about the general nature of reality is, I think, obvious.

(Winch 1958: 9–10)

On Winch's reading, then, the professor's two hands do not prove the existence of the external world but simply remind us of the common meaning of the term 'external world'. For Winch, the point that Moore, replicating what Hume had done more than 150 years earlier (see above, p. 19), was making was the opposite of the one Moore thought he was making. This, of course, raises the issue of the nature of language, which Winch deals with in the manner of the later Wittgenstein. That is, he understands language to be a set of rules governing the usage of words that gain and change their meanings according to the practical uses to which they are put. The result is that, within any linguistic community, people necessarily know a lot about not just the language they use but also about their society. Thus language is not simply a set of linguistic rules but also a veritable encyclopedia of social knowlege which can be used to give meaning to or rescue what would otherwise be communication failures. This means that even the following extraordinary product description helpfully provided by the Chinese manufacturer of my power drill may be made meaningful – please try:

BB-DRI09 scrics of impact drill are double insulate electric tools.They are ariven by singlephase motor and are induced by appear of gears, they compact siaccture a dvanced technology, Large cut power, little noise, light weight,high effcie ney and convenient mainte rance are their advantages. This series at impact drill are suitable to use an metal plastic and wood, ete; if the speciat acces sorles attach.they can used as motorrscrew driver, motorteveT.Gastling sand machinery. Sand polishing machinery. So they are ideat electric tools in artwork.

There is, then, something to be said for this aspect of Winch's argument, but what are its consequences in terms of research strategy?

Conclusion

The argument for the equal and intertwined dependence of meaning on linguistic rules and the social context within which it is used has some radical consequences for research strategy. The first two follow from the argument that not knowing a language means that one cannot understand the society that produces that language. The first is that externalist approaches are pointless because not only is the knowledge they seek already available to insiders but it is also impossible to make up for the absence of such insider knowledge from the outside. The second rules out one of Weber's and indeed Durkheim's principal modes of external validation, namely comparative analysis, since each combination of rules and social life is unique and therefore incomparable. The third follows from the argument that to speak a language, especially as a native speaker, is to know a society. And it is that as social life and therefore the world in general is created for us in language, it is therefore both visible in, and readily understandable through, our participation in its discourses. The result is that, for Winch and social constructionists more generally, the goal of research cannot be the production of theory because theory is unnecessary.

5 Looking as work

The various sets of metatheoretical assumptions and the research strategy templates outlined in the preceding chapters constitute sets of rules as to how to go about understanding social life. Rules imply techniques of implementation and such techniques imply tools, materials and workplaces; that is, the life of the mind is externalized through, and in a dialogue with, various things. The sociologist of science Bruno Latour (1993) has argued, convincingly in my view, that because of such relationships not only can minds and things only be understood when they are considered together, but also that what minds and things produce in the case of the arts and manufactures or discover in the case of the natural and social sciences must also be understood as physical/mental 'hybrids' or 'quasi-objects'.

Latour, whose basic metatheoretical stance is an elusive variant of a Winch-type social constructionism, uses this insight as part of what appears to be a partial rapprochement with ontological realism – the thingness of instruments etc. is granted, as suggested by the term 'quasi-objects' and his wonderful idea of the 'parliament of things'. However, the thingness of the human side of sociality continues to be refused. Irrespective of my own views of this refusal, I have found Latour's work useful in suggesting a way to convey a much less contentious point, namely that social theory is not simply an intellectual means of manipulating visualities but also a process of *work* involving things, namely tools, materials, instruments, and workplaces. The nature of the tools involved – books, archives, paper, and writing or calculating instruments of one kind or another – is obvious. According to some sets of rules, namely rationalism and realism, the theories produced by using these tools may be applied directly to the materials of interest. According to others, especially empiricism and interpretivism, more specialized instruments are required. In the case of empiricism, examples of such instruments would be questionnaires, surveys, panel studies, and their associated statistical techniques. In the case of interpretivism, one would need to add interviews and various observation techniques to the foregoing (for a fascinating account of the history of interviewing and its associated technologies, see Lee 2004). These differences, in turn, mean that theory is produced in a wide variety of workplace settings which, when approached archaeologically, can tell us much of interest about the variety of ways in which theory is produced. For this reason, this chapter will consist of a series of excerpts from accounts of such workplaces, specifically the study, the reading group, the research centre, the knowledge corporation, and the 'field' (for reasons that will become apparent, I have reserved the discussion of the academic department to the conclusion of the book as a whole). The excerpts that follow will be linked by a simple commentary that is intended to provide just enough comment to enable the reader to appreciate the range of practices involved in theoretical work and therefore to begin to visualize the actual work practices associated with the abstract rules for sociological looking and their associated methodologies that have already been discussed.

The archetypal site of theory production and use is of course the study, which it seems was first invented as a distinctively private space during the Renaissance (Thornton 1998) and therefore at the beginning of the metatheoretical history outlined in the preceding chapters. The study is the theorist's equivalent of the artist's studio, or the priest's holy of holies. Sometimes a great deal of thought and effort is put into getting the atmosphere just right, although seldom as much as in the case of the central character in what in the present context is Joris-Karl Huysman's aptly titled novel of 1884, *Against Nature*:

> In the end he decided to have his walls bound like books, in heavy smooth Morocco leather, using skins from the Cape glazed by huge plaques of steel under a powerful press.
>
> Once the panelling had been decorated, he had the mouldings and the tall skirting-boards painted with a dark indigo blue enamel, similar to that used by coach-builders on the panels of carriages; the slightly domed ceiling, also covered in Morocco leather, displayed, like a vast sky-light framed in its orange mounting, a circle of sky of royal blue silk, in whose centre silver seraphims – embroidered long ago, for an ancient cope, by the Weavers' Guild of Cologne – winged their way swiftly upward.
>
> When all this was in place, the entire effect, at night, blended together, becoming tempered and settled; the blues of the panelling, now stabilized, were sustained and as though warmed by the oranges, while these in their turn maintained their integrity, being supported and, in a sense, enlivened by the compelling proximity of the blues. As for the furniture, Des Esseintes did not have to undertake any lengthy researches, inasmuch as books and rare flowers were to be that room's only luxury; later he planned to dec-

orate the still-bare panelling with a few drawings or paintings, but
for now he contented himself with installing shelving and book-
cases of ebony on most of the walls; he scattered wild-animal skins
and blue fox pelts on the parquet and, alongside a massive fifteenth-
century money-changer's table, he placed some deep, winged arm-
chairs, and an old wrought-iron stand taken from a chapel, one of
those antique lecterns on which, in the past, the deacon placed the
Antiphonary, and which now held one of the weighty in-folios ...

The casement windows, whose bluish, crackled panes, studded
with the bulging, gold-flecked irregularities of bottle glass, cut off
the view of the countryside and allowed only a deceptive light to
penetrate, were in their turn hung with draperies made out of
antique stoles, whose darkened, smoky gold threadwork was
quenched by the almost lifeless russet of the weave.

(Huysmans 1998: 14–15)

Much more often theorists have had to achieve the requisite serenity
and sense of self-importance mentally and without the help of leather-
pannelled walls and 'rare flowers'. What follows is a description of Marx's
study in London's Soho written by a Prussian government spy in 1852:

As a father and husband, Marx, in spite of his wild and restless
character, is the gentlest and mildest of men. Marx lives in one of
the worst, therefore one of the cheapest quarters of London. He
occupies two rooms. The one looking out on the street is the salon,
and the bedroom is at the back. In the whole apartment there is
not one clean and solid piece of furniture. Everything is broken,
tattered and torn, with a half inch of dust over everything and the
greatest disorder everywhere. In the middle of the salon there is a
large old-fashioned table covered with an oilcloth, and on it there
lie manuscripts, books and newspapers, as well as the children's
toys, the rags and tatters of his wife's sewing basket, several cups
with broken rims, knives, forks, lamps, an inkpot, tumblers, Dutch
clay pipes, tobacco ash – in a word, everything topsy-turvy, and all
on the same table. A seller of second-hand goods would be
ashamed to give away such a remarkable collection of odds and
ends.

When you enter Marx's room smoke and tobacco fumes make
your eyes water so much that for a moment you seem to be groping
about in a cavern, but gradually, as you grow accustomed to the
fog, you can make out certain objects which distinguish themselves from the surrounding haze. Everything is dirty, and covered
with dust, so that to sit down becomes a thoroughly dangerous
business. Here is a chair with only three legs, on another chair the

children are playing at cooking – this chair happens to have four legs. This is the one which is offered to the visitor, but the children's cooking has not been wiped away; and if you sit down, you risk a pair of trousers.

(McLennan 1996: 268–9)

Sometimes the physical conditions are even worse, as in the case of the prison cells that Antonio Gramsci had to work in during the 1930s and Tony Negri, one of the authors of *Empire* (2001), a recent and very unlikely social theory bestseller, has to work in today. However, even when the physical conditions are far better, as is most often the case, the psychological conditions in the study can make them far from comfortable places to work in, as in Max Weber's case:

All available evidence then, suggests that Max Weber, a man whom his contemporaries frequently described as the possessor of a 'volcanic' temper, spent the eleven years between his arrival at his father's home in 1886 and his father's death in 1897 accumulating a vast but inexpressible loathing for this man and a deep sympathy for his maltreated mother. If we make the elementary hypothesis that a man so consumed by emotions he cannot express vocally must express them in some other way, we are led to investigate the relationship between these inexpressible, but clearly quite conscious, passions of Max Weber and the apparently non-familial dimensions of his life in those years: his scholarship and his politics. For both in his manner of work and in the values inspiring the results of that work, Weber betrayed the hatred that conventional inhibition forebade him to unleash.

One cannot possibly produce as much and as well as Weber did in the years before 1897 without enormous self-discipline, and it is therefore not surprising to find that as early as his year of study in Berlin (1884–5) Weber subjected himself to a ruthless work schedule. In the following semester in Gottingen, 'he continues the rigid work discipline, regulates his life by the clock, divides the daily routine into exact sections for the various subjects, saves in his way, by feeding himself evenings in his room with a pound of raw chopped beef and four fried eggs.' One can only infer that, in the course of transferring his loyalty and sympathy from his father to his mother while at Strassburg, Weber had taken over his mother's Huguenot asceticism. Certainly, the adoption of such a severely repressive asceticism functioned as a means of retaining his mother's good will … the 'danger of becoming comfortable' was for Weber a lifelong peril, emanating from his father's nature, to understand the intimate relationship between Puritanical work morality and antagonism to his father's authority in his life.

(Mitzman 1969: 47–9, references removed)

Since the 1960s, voluntary but typically invitation-only (no people likely to disagree too much are invited) reading and study groups have become very common sites for theoretical discussion. The idea is to overcome the isolation of the study and/or the absence of congenial departmental colleagues by assembling a collection of kindred spirits from different institutions, setting some reading or asking someone to give a presentation, providing some alcohol and crisps, and then waiting for the sparks to fly. This can be a very productive site and of course such sites have existed for millennia as in the case of ancient Greece. Perhaps the most famous and influential of such groups in the twentieth century were the Vienna Circle, which has already been discussed, and the College de Socologie, which met regularly in Paris between 1937 and 1939. Denis Hollier (1988: p. vii; see also Pearce 2003, 2005) has described the College as exemplifying 'theory's novelistic side'. Certainly, the combination of the personalities centrally involved (today, the best known are Georges Bataille, Roger Caillois, and Michel Leiris) with the Durkheimian and Surrealist ideas in which they were interested produced some very wild sparks indeed, notably the one that led to the group's disintegration. This was the suggestion that they could prevent war by, like the Aztecs in ancient Mexico, sacrificing one or more of their number in order to restore the sacred status of humanity – somewhat reassuringly the problem was not the lack of a willing victim but of someone prepared to perform the act.

Here is the founding declaration of the College:

1   As soon as particular importance is attributed to the study of social structures, one sees that the few results obtained in this realm by science not only are generally unknown but, moreover, directly contradict current ideas on these subjects. These results appear at first extremely promising and open unexpected viewpoints for the study of human behavior. But they remain timid and incomplete, on the one hand, because science has been too limited to the analysis of so-called primitive societies, while ignoring modern societies; and on the other hand, because the discoveries made have not modified the assumptions and attitudes of research as profoundly as might be expected. It even seems that there are obstacles of a particular nature opposed to the development of an understanding of the vital elements of society. The necessarily contagious and *activist* character of the representations that this work brings to light seems responsible for this.

2   It follows that there is good reason for those who contemplate
    following investigations as far as possible in this direction, to
    develop a moral community, different in part from that ordin-
    arily uniting scholars and bound, precisely, to the virulent
    character of the realm studied and of the laws that little by
    little are revealed to govern it. This community, nonetheless,
    is as free of access as the established scientific community, and
    anyone can contribute a personal point of view to it, without
    regard for the particular concern inducing one to get a more
    precise knowledge of the essential aspects of social existence.
    No matter what one's origin and goal, this preoccupation
    alone is considered to be enough to create the necessary ties
    for common action.

3   The precise object of the contemplated activity can take the
    name of Sacred Sociology, implying the study of all manifest-
    ations of social existence where the active presence of the
    sacred is clear. It intends to establish in this way the points of
    coincidence between the fundamental obsessive tendencies of
    individual psychology and the principal structures that govern
    social organization and are in command of its revolutions.

                                                    (Hollier 1988: 5)

The less novelistic side of theory production is represented by today's
burgeoning number of research centres. These are typically adjuncts of university departments that have been set up to receive the large sums of
money that governments and charities or foundations are nowadays sometimes prepared to put into social research when they need, or think they
need, certain kinds of information to help with policy making or governance. Many of these centres never become more than letterheads, but
others have been around for a long time and working in them can be just
like working in a well-established corporation. This is a description of work
life in one of the most famous research centres:

[At] the Institute of Social Research [ISR] of the University of
Michigan ... [t]here [are] many different projects at varying stages
of development ... housed in the same building. A project director
can always find other project directors to talk to – some who have
moved through whatever phase the project is currently in, others
who are approaching it, all of them with curiosity and interest and
competence in research. Similarly, research assistants can find
counterparts from other projects; they can gripe about their jobs
and their bosses and the idiocy of their assignments and can return
to work with fresh perspectives.

                                        (Riesman and Watson 1964: 256)

However, because much of the money on which research centres depend is soft and short term, the working environment in such a centre can sometimes be rather dispiriting. And this may be so despite the fame and ability of the project leaders, as in the case, ironically, of the Sociability Project led by two of the most famous American sociologists of the postwar period, David Riesman, the author of the *Lonely Crowd* (one of the best-selling sociology books of all time), and William Foote Whyte, the author of *Street Corner Society* (the classic participant observation study):

> The Sociability Project was quartered in the Family Study Center and, during the year 1955–1956 ... The building had an empty, waiting quality; there was no nucleus of people to gather for a coffee break or for lunch, just the waiting desks and typewriters ...
> (Riesman and Watson 1964: 255)

Not only are some research centres such as the ISR run like corporations but some actually are corporations, so-called 'knowledge corporations'. The best known of these is the Rand Corporation, where Francis Fukuyama, the author of yet another best-selling work of social theory, *The End of History*, had his study. This an extract from Rand's mission statement:

> Our job is to help improve policy and decision making through research and analysis. We do that in many ways. Sometimes, we develop new knowledge to inform decision makers without suggesting any specific course of action. Often, we go further by spelling out the range of available options and by analysing their relative advantages and disadvantages. On many other occasions, we find the analysis so compelling that we advance specific policy recommendations. In all cases, we serve the public interest by widely disseminating our research findings.
>
> Today, RAND's work is exceptionally diverse. We now assist all branches of the U.S. military community, and we apply our expertise to social and international issues as well. For example: We partnered with health experts throughout the United States to identify specific health care improvements to help millions of children with asthma.

> RAND collaborated with other research groups to study how anti-drug laws help prevent illicit drug use by teenagers. The Department of Labor asked RAND to examine how economic conditions affect the availability of health insurance for workers. We're now working with the White House Office of Science and Technology Policy to better understand how technology can reduce greenhouse gas emissions. In all of our work, we strive for

the highest levels of quality, objectivity, and innovation – hallmarks that have earned us a prominent reputation throughout the world. Our commitment to these standards will continue to define our work into the future.

Corporate mission: RAND is a nonprofit institution that helps improve policy and decision making through research and analysis ...

Employee Statistics: The full- and part-time staff of more than 1,600 represents diversity in work experience; political and ideological outlook; race, gender, and ethnicity; and academic training. Eighty-five percent of the research staff hold advanced degrees, with more than sixty-five percent having earned Ph.D's or M.D.'s.

Locations: RAND has four principal locations, Santa Monica, California; Arlington, Virginia (just outside Washington, D.C.); Pittsburgh, Pennsylvania; and Rand Europe headquarters in Leiden, The Netherlands. RAND Europe also has offices in Berlin, Germany, and Cambridge, the United Kingdom. RAND's other offices in the United States include Council for Aid to Education in New York City and several smaller sites.

Finally, in addition to one or more of the workplaces already specified, many theorists also work in what, for some at least, could be appropriately described as the 'outside world' but in fact is almost universally termed 'the field'. Sometimes fieldwork can be boring and very tiring, as Howard Newby, the sociologist who is presently the head of the Higher Education Funding Council for England (HEFCE), discovered when he was literally in the fields doing the research for his study of English farmworkers, *The Deferential Worker*:

Doing the survey was an experience that involved a number of sequential stages, familiar to most researchers. At the beginning the dominant emotion was one of elation that the real world seemed roughly to correspond to how one had envisaged it; one conveniently overlooked the unexpected but bored friends with anecdotes about how abstractly conceived ideas were unfolding before one's eyes. Then the novelty began to wear off. Respondents began to settle into a pattern, and interviewing became a routine. Eventually a certain tedium set in; enthusiasm could only be raised with an effort, and asking the same question for the two-hundredth time became a hard slog. One longed for an eccentric respondent to disrupt the established pattern. By the end I had interviewed 71 farmers and 233 farm workers, each interview lasting on average half an hour for the farmers and one and a half hours for the farmworkers. It was an exhausting experience, both physically and emotionally. Wandering into people's homes and asking them a series of sometimes intimate questions was not something which I found came naturally to me. I would become quite nervous immediately before knocking on someone's door, and on the few occasions when it was slammed in my face or I was the object of abuse I became quite rattled and gripped by agonies of self-doubt. What right had I to ask all these questions anyway? What was it all for? Was it all worth it? Somehow Galtung and Blalock had not had all this trouble.

(Newby 1977: 117)

On other occasions and fortunately, fieldwork can be a lot of fun, as the researchers on the ill-fated Sociability Study described earlier discovered on their better days:

We found in the days following a party [only attended for research purposes, of course] that we would suddenly be reminded of 'forgotten' episodes by fresh encounters with the persons or ideas or places that had figured in the 'forgotten' conversation. In the early days of November, we did not reach this generalization, but we did conclude that memory was more adequate as a tool for the study of episodes than for the study of sequence and chronology. After two weeks of practice in observing ourselves and discussion of ways of standardizing our write-ups of episodes, we moved into the field. Each assistant made an effort in November and December to collect observations of the sociability of his own group of subjects, including the SSA students. Each created his own means of gaining access to sociable interaction. Bob spent two evenings in the apartment of a group of airline hostesses, noting interaction among the girls and also between the girls and various young men who dropped in. Joan set up one evening of bridge and one evening of Scrabble, recording interaction both during and after the games. Al joined the group of law students who met for lunch, eating with them several times a week. Andi got herself invited home for Thanksgiving by one dating couple and, in addition, met separately with them and with one other subject-defining her activity as that of participant-observer in the development of friendship rather than as observation-from-the-outside. The project director reviewed the reports as they came in, made suggestions to each individual about ways of improving and standardizing his reporting, and began to think about ways of analysing the observations.

(Riesman and Watson 1964: 254)

However, not even such 'breakthroughs' were sufficient to lift the gloom that seemed to have descended on this study of people having a good time:

> This list of accomplishments may seem meager, and, indeed, we were dissatisfied with it. However, it appeared that an immense amount of time was consumed, first, in making arrangements to be present at events which would permit us to observe the sociable behavior of our subjects and, second, in writing up reports of the observations. In addition, staff members were still working to transcribe the long interviews previously obtained; numerous staff meetings were held in which the theoretical concerns of the project were given attention; and demands of the academic half time of the assistants were implacable. Whatever the reasons or excuses, it remains true that Foote and Riesman were evaluating the success of the enterprise in terms of the written materials; these were inadequate in quantity and poor in quality.
>
> (Riesman and Watson 1964: 254)

Fortunately, there are also occasions when the exaltation that is part of 'theory's novelistic side' may be experienced in the field and very much with nature rather than against it. This is made particularly clear in the following extract from the conclusion to the structuralist theorist Claude Levi Strauss's otherwise generally rather melancholy study, *Tristes Tropiques*:

> It was in Asia, many years later, that – for myself, at any rate – the problems suggested by this book were to find their solution. In September 1950 I was in a Mogh village in the Chittagong hill tracts. For some days I had been watching the women as they went each morning to the temple with food for the *bonzes* [monks]. During the siesta hours I listened to the strokes on the gong which punctuated the prayers, and to the children's voices softly intoning the Burmese alphabet. The *kyong* stood at the edge of the village on the top of a little wooded hillock like those with which Tibetan painters like to garnish their far distances. At its foot was the *jldi*, or pagoda. In that poor village it was no more than a circular earthen construction which rose from the ground in seven concentric stages, rising step by step, in a square enclosure trellised with bamboo ...
>
> On the fourth side stood the temple itself ... The floor was made up of large sections of bamboo, split down the middle and plaited together. Shiny from the continual movement of bare feet, it yielded to the touch as softly as any carpet. A peaceful barn-like atmosphere prevailed and there was a smell of hay. The simple,

spacious room might have been an abandoned hay-loft; and when combined with the courtesy of the two *bonzes*, erect, with their two straw pallets on bedsteads, and with the touching care and devotion which had been lavished on the assemblage or manufacture of all the accessories of worship, all this brought me nearer than ever before to having some idea of the meaning of a sanctuary ...

Between Marxist criticism which sets Man free from his first chains, and Buddhist criticism, which completes that liberation, there is neither opposition nor contradiction, (the Marxist teaches that the apparent significance of Man's condition will vanish the moment he agrees to enlarge the object that he has under consideration.) Marxism and Buddhism are doing the same thing, but at different levels. The passage between the two extremes is guaranteed by all those advances in knowledge that our race has accomplished in the last two thousand years ...

(Levi-Strauss 1961: 410–12)

Conclusion

In sum, even in the narrow context of the workplace (the wider context will be outlined in Part 2) theoretical work involves combining thought with varying methodological skills, techniques, institutions and objects, including social ones. The visible differences between tools, workplaces and combinations of them are significant because, as the material side of Latour's hybrid quasi-objects, they may be read as archaeological evidence for the existence of the otherwise invisible but clearly differentiated sets of ontological and epistemological assumptions that explain why different schools of social-scientific practitioners produce pictures of social life that vary as much as those produced by different schools of artists. Assuming that all varieties of theoretical work are, in part at least, carried out in libraries, studies, and with or without participation in reading groups, what appears to vary as a consequence of the nature of the sets of ontological and epistemological assumptions governing the theoretical work produced in particular sites is the nature of the primary workplace and the particular combination of sites in which the work is carried out. Thus, the following sets of indicators and assumptions may be distinguished:

Where the workplace is the study alone, the theory produced is likely to rest on rationalistic/idealist assumptions. This is because reason or the capacity to think without contradicting oneself is considered to be sufficient for the discovery of the truth.

Where the primary workplace is the research centre or the know-ledge corporation, the theory produced is most likely to rest on empiricist assumptions. This is because extensive and accurate observation is considered to be necessary for theory generation and this requires large numbers of assistants to gather and analyse the data.

Where the workplace is both the study and the field, the theory produced is likely to rest on interpretivist assumptions. This is because, although reason is regarded as sufficient to define what needs to understood, interviews and fieldwork more generally are considered to be necessary because the point is to understand social life from the point of view of the actors involved.

Where the workplaces are multiple and include the study, various archives, the historical and area studies sections of the library, and sometimes the field too, the theory produced is likely to rest on realist assumptions. This is because, although reason is again regarded as sufficient to define what has to understood, historical and/or comparative evidence as well as material gathered in the field are required in order to model the relationships of interest and to test the explanations that have been generated in the study.

It is very tempting to read the ordering of the earlier account of theo-retical workplaces (from the study to the knowledge corporation) and that of the changing nature of the hybrid quasi-objects that they represent (from the means of production associated with craftwork to those associated with mass production) and produce (from histories and ethnographies to surveys and, most expensive of all, longitudinal or panel studies) as suggesting a connection between the increasing expense of theory production and its increasingly empiricist and conservative character. And indeed I am not going to resist this temptation very strenuously because it seems a reason-able generalization on the basis of my experience. However, it is certainly not an entirely safe generalization as regards either the past or the present. This is because, on the one hand, many empiricist and conservative works have been produced in studies or emerged from study groups such as those who met during the 1960s and 1970s in the United States to discuss the works of the political philosopher Leo Strauss and in so doing generated the ideas known today as neo-Conservativism. On the other hand, the Rand Corporation's former employee, Francis Fukuyama, for example, is an avowed Hegelian who does not base his theorizations on survey research. Moreover, politically progressive (that is, for me, egalitarian) use may be made of survey data or longitudinal studies relating to, for example, poverty, inequality, health, time budgets, or whatever (for an excellent set of examples of such use, see Gregg *et al.* 2003). Indeed it should be said that it is a desire to see politically progressive use made of such data that very often motivates its producers. However, because the data so assiduously and expensively gathered have often been produced in response to policy questions that politicians wish to appear to be taking seriously but do not really want to know the answers to, the data are also often not as useful for theoretical purposes as they might be. This is because they do not include answers to the further questions that might make them theoretically pertinent – for example it is of little theoretical use to ask about the extent and causes of poverty if questions are not also asked about the extent and causes of wealth concentration.

Part Two
The Social Life of Theory

6 Towards a realist reflexivity

In the preceding Part, I showed how different sets of metatheoretical assumptions determine how practitioners go about their research, which aspects of social life they produce theories of, and, therefore, what sort of pictures they generate of social life. Since the points at issue between the different metatheoretical positions are inherently undecidable and the task of understanding social life is so difficult, the only way to advance the sociological enterprise is by ensuring that all positions are allowed to flourish and interact with one another, even if the importance and difficulty of the quest means that tensions are endemic in social science workplaces and communities with the result that quite bitter conflicts may occasionally occur between colleagues. Indeed, I am convinced that such conflicts are a condition of intellectual progress, because there is a sense in which to pick an intellectual fight with someone represents a mark of respect for that person's position, a taking seriously of the challenges that the person's work represents. What makes me say this is a worry I have about the present apparently pacific state of the disciplines of which social theory is a part. On the one hand, it is good that we no longer have to work amidst the theory wars that marked the last four decades of the twentieth century (conflict versus consensus; action versus system; agency versus structure; postmodernism versus modernism), because we are saved from the pressure to take sides and are free to draw inspiration from all corners of the theoretical universe. But, on the other hand, given that it cannot be the case that all theories are correct, it is not so good if, as I sometimes fear, these wars have ended in a combination of banal, so-called syntheses, and a more general partitioning or balkanization of the different theoretical camps that, in part at least, is maintained by the passive-aggressive strategem of the studied or motivated neglect of competing positions. I have written at length elsewhere (Woodiwiss 2001) about the contribution of a particular mode of theorizing to this state of affairs and how it may be superceded, so I will spend no further time on these issues here. I mention them only in order to indicate the general nature of the reasons why I will adopt a rather more partisan stance in Part Two as I try to demonstrate what is involved in making a theoretical intervention.

In Part One, because of the logical necessity of metatheoretical tolerance, I provided what I hope is a fair if not an entirely neutral account of the different sets of assumptions and research strategies as well as examples of their use. By contrast, in this Part, because of the equal necessity of contestation for social-scientific advance, I will demonstrate how to make a particular kind of theoretical intervention by developing an alternative to the currently predominant conception of reflexivity and using this alternative to provide a critical account of some of the major developments in social theory over the past 50 years or so (for some recent and far more affirmative accounts of these developments, see Alexander 2003; Friedland and Mohr 2004; Lemert 2004). In so doing, I will be drawing on the results of my own theoretical and empirical work. The reader will notice that, because of my increased personal stake in the outcome, my writing will carry more emotion and become more rhetorical as I try to convince the reader to see things my way through my choice of adjectives and the increased frequency of evaluative statements. In what follows, just as I decided to engage in a radical rather than milder form of critique for reasons of pedagogical clarity, I will deploy these rhetorical stratagems in a somewhat exaggerated fashion in order to make their use more noticeable. It is therefore important to say that, were I not engaged in a pedagogical exercise, I would be doing my best to minimize the obviousness of my use of such stratagems since their overuse can be counter-productive. To theorize is, as Frederick Nietzsche put it, to exercise a 'will to power'. The question I wish to address, however, is 'Is it simply the theorist's own will to power?'

Rescuing reflexivity

In my view, and in order to make my own position clear, Durkheim was not only being a good realist but also correct when he declared (see above, pp. 46–7) that the foundational, substantive ontological assumption of sociology was that social life was a *'sui generis'* object or 'a natural product, like organisms or plants, which are born, which grow and develop through some internal necessity.' Indeed it is hard to think of a stronger way of making the basic realist ontological point, namely that the social exists independently of human thought about it. Durkheim was also being an acute defender of realism when, on the same occasion, and presumably referring to John Locke's notion of the 'social contract', he said that what had 'radically prevented the establishment of sociology' was the alternative assumption that 'men began to live together because they found that it was useful and good: society is an invention which they thought up in order to better their condition a little.' Again, it is hard to think of a keener appreciation of the source of what I too regard as the principal threat to sociological realism, namely a humanist ontology; that is, the belief basic to interpretivism/social constructivism, namely that individual human beings are the ultimate and only social stuff.

What, of course, Durkheim could not have known was that such a humanist ontology would continue to undermine sociological progress into the twenty-first century. Like the other classical theorists, Durkheim was profoundly self-conscious or, as we would say today, 'reflexive' about his reasoning. He would, therefore, have been extremely surprised, not to say shocked, to discover that one of the most important conduits for the forces that have continued to subvert his project should be the recognition of the importance of 'reflexivity' to effective theoretical practice.

The basic meaning of the term 'reflexivity' is the capacity to reflect on one's thoughts or actions and alter what one thinks and/or does in the light of such reflection. In this broad sense it has always been part of intellectual or social life in that human beings, whether as individuals or groups, have long been aware of their capacity to reflect on why they think or act in the way that they do, and they have valued this capacity as a means of improving or at least changing themselves and their relationships to their surroundings. In the present study we have already encountered some of the most profound products of the exercise of this capacity in the formulation of the various metatheoretical positions that have been discussed. The problem, however, is that over the past 20 or so years many sociologists and especially those who regard themselves primarily as theorists have been so impressed by the profundity of reflexivity's achievements that an accidental, largely unconscious but widespread solipsism has resulted in the confusion of the ideas that are in the theorist's mind not only with their own ideas but also with knowledge of the world. The result has been that an intellectual climate has been created wherein talking and writing about theory has come to be regarded as an adequate substitute for engaging in research and making theory. Consequently, humanistic idealisms of many weird and not so wonderful kinds have flourished – and this to the degree that society itself has been pictured as some kind of humanoid being that has become reflexive and therefore dissolved itself back into its individual parts:

> What happens, analysts like Beck and Giddens ask, when modernity begins to reflect on itself? What happens when modernization, understanding its own excesses and vicious spiral of destructive subjugation (of inner, outer and social nature) begins to take itself as an object of reflection? This new self-reflexivity of modernity, on this view, would be a lot more than the belated victory of 'free will' over the forces of 'fate' or 'determinism'. It would instead

be a development immanent to the modernization process itself. It would be a condition of, at a certain historical point, the development of functional prerequisites for further modernization. In the late twentieth century, if modernization as economic growth is to be possible, the workforce must acquire substantial information-processing abilities and thus must be highly educated. The framework of problem-solving, questioning and the like involved in this education process is also a condition of acquisition of the sort of knowledge that can be turned as rational critique upon the 'system' itself. If modernization presupposes increased individualization, then these individuals – less controlled by tradition and convention – will be increasingly free also to be in heterodox opposition to the dystopic consequences of modernization. And indeed this is the sort of distinction that reflexive modernization makes in regard to 'simple' modernization ... In brief, if simple modernization means subjugation, then reflexive modernization involves the empowerment of subjects. If simple modernization gives us Foucault's scenario of atomization, normalization and individuation, then the reflexive counterpart opens up a *genuine individualization*, opens up positive possibilities of autonomous subjectivity in regard to our natural, social and psychic environments.

(Beck *et al.* 1994: 112–13, emphasis added)

I have many problems with the ideas summarized in this passage, but two are the most significant in the present context. First, there is their anthropomorphism (treating society as if it was a human being), which leads to the representation of the history of the last 50 or so years as the transformation of a voracious and supposedly humanoid monster, modernity, into a community of lots of nice little persons – 'genuine' individuals – thanks to the monster gaining the capacity to be reflexive. Second, there is the extraordinary idea that the risk assessments that pervade contemporary advanced capitalist societies have any kinship with intellectual reflexivity – the former are generally a means of minimizing or avoiding responsibilities, whereas the latter is otherwise always and correctly presented as a strategy for uncovering and taking responsibilities.

Taking reflexivity seriously, however, need not lead to anthropomorphism and the solipsism that seems to be both its cause and consequence. On the contrary, as Bourdieu and Wacquant (1992: Chapter 3) have argued so eloquently, reflexivity is essential if one is to escape repeating common sense ideas or what, following Foucault, they call the 'unthought', and so also avoid repeating the biases, prejudices and preconceptions that result from and reinforce inequalities in the disposition of power. In short, practising such a mode of reflexivity is essential if you wish to become critically aware, not simply of your own assumptions and preconceptions, but also of the interrelationships between knowledge and power that obtain in your field of interest or expertise, let alone incorporate these insights and out-sights into your practice – if, in sum, you wish to be able to avoid confusing the thoughts that are in your mind with your *own* thought, as well as with knowledge of society.

In order to help the reader attain such awareness, the remainder of this Part is divided into three sections. This chapter will focus on how the means for gaining an awareness of the unthought were developed. Chapter 7 will outline how the effectiveness of these means was greatly reduced as a consequence of many of those who regard themselves as theorists losing sight of social structure in general and of the class structure in particulary and focusing instead on the issue of identity. In so doing, it will also suggest how the critical effectiveness of reflexivity might be restored and used to understand the specific character of the unthought that currently threatens the sociological enterprise. Chapter 8 will outline how the ever-changing nature of social life may already have initiated this process of restoration by showing how our developing understanding of globalization has again fore-grounded the need for an enhanced understanding of social structure.

The three main and thoroughly legitimate reasons for engaging in reflexive activity are: to spot gaps and jumps in one's reasoning, whether they are caused by abstract or substantive assumptions and/or biases; to check the consistency of one's reasoning; and to understand the relations between theoretical work and power. Each of these reasons is equally legitimate, but there has been a marked tendency for the first to be a more common motivation than the second and third with the result that many recent theorizations have been inconsistent, even incoherent, and testaments more to their author's political naivety than to their scientificity. The interrelated nature of these points will now be illustrated in the course of a brief account of the development of the sociological understanding of the nature of the relations between power and knowledge, which will also introduce some significant instances of postclassical theorizing.

Power and knowledge

It is possible to discern two somewhat different approaches to the power/knowledge issue in Marx's work. Jorge Larrain (1979) has usefully labelled them the positive and negative concepts of ideology, and the differences between them neatly illustrate the general point that developments with respect to evidence lead to changes in the nature or definitions of concepts. The negative concept of ideology was first deployed in *The German Ideology* in order to explain why a set of ideas that were, in Marx's view, so obviously mistaken as those produced by Hegel should have for a time been so widely believed in the German-speaking world. Marx famously summarized his explanation as follows: 'the ruling ideas of a period are in every epoch the ideas of the ruling class.' In other words, thanks to their possession of more leisure, education and money, those who control the means of economic production also control the means of intellectual production either through their own efforts or the efforts of those they employ or otherwise support. The result is that the ruled both think about their behaviour and act in ways that advance the interests of their rulers rather than their own and in so doing exhibit a false consciousness.

The positive concept of ideology was first deployed after 20 or so years of further work in *Capital*, wherein it is understood as a visual effect produced by what Marx termed the 'fetishism of commodities':

> A commodity is therefore a mysterious thing, simply because in it the social character of men's labour appears to them as an objective character stamped upon the product of that labour; because the relation of the producers to the sum total of their own labour is presented to them as a social relation, existing not between themselves, but between the products of their labour. This is the reason why the products of labour become commodities, social things whose qualities are at the same time perceptible and imperceptible by the senses. In the same way the light from an object is perceived by us not as the subjective excitation of our optic nerve, but as the objective form of something outside the eye itself. But, in the act of seeing, there is at all events, an actual passage of light from one thing to another, from the external object to the eye. There is a physical relation between physical things. But it is different with commodities. There, the existence of the things qua commodities, and the value-relation between the products of labour which stamps them as commodities, have absolutely no connexion with their physical properties and with the material relations arising therefrom. There it is a definite social relation between men, that assumes, in their eyes, the fantastic form of a relation between things. In order, therefore, to find an analogy, we must have recourse to the mist-enveloped regions of the religious world. In that world the productions of the human brain appear as independent beings endowed with life, and entering into relation both with one another and the human race. So it is in the world of commodities with the products of men's hands. This I call the fetishism which attaches itself to the products of labour, so soon as they are produced as commodities, and which is therefore inseparable from the production of commodities.

> This fetishism of commodities has its origin, as the foregoing analysis has already shown, in the peculiar social character of the labour that produces them.
>
> (Marx 1965: 71)

In order to understand this passage one has to know what a fetish is. Baldly put, a fetish is a result that is mistaken for a process. Anthropologists have taught us that the curative powers ascribed to a shaman's fetish doll in fact arise not because of the properties intrinsic to such objects but rather because of the psychological effects of the traditions and rituals within which the dolls are used. Likewise, psychoanalysis has taught us that the erotic power of, say, black leather clothing is not intrinsic to it, but arises because of the particular circumstances under which responsive individuals' desires were shaped. In the case of capitalist society, the market is omnipresent which results in everything, including labour power, appearing to be a commodity whose price is determined by its value in the market. The process that is thereby lost sight of is the exploitation that follows from the disadvantageous position that, lacking the means to provide for their own subsistence, workers find themselves in when they present themselves for work. Although the consequence is again that the ruled are in the thrall of a false conciousness, Marx also seems to be making the point that capital's rule is unquestioned not so much because people are brainwashed but more as a consequence of the structuring of their lives and their consequently apparently willing participation in the ordinary activities of capitalist societies, especially buying and selling. Thus the rule of capital, like that of the Hegel's slave owners, depends on the nature of the true source of its power over labour remaining unacknowledged. Moreover, again as in the case of Hegel's master/slave dialectic, the fetishism of commodities is understood to refer to an inherently unstable relationship except that the source of this instability is not the denial of the subordinate's humanity but a structural contradiction as Marx explained in a passage that has already been quoted (see above, p. 42):

> At a certain stage of their development, the material productive forces of society come in conflict with the existing relations of production, or – what is but a legal expression for the same thing – with the property relations within which they have been at work hitherto. From forms of development of the productive forces these relations turn into their fetters. Then begins an epoch of social revolution. With the change of the economic foundation the entire immense superstructure is more or less rapidly transformed.

The obvious questions left unanswered by both the negative and positive concepts of ideology are: 'How exactly is working class acceptance of capital's rule achieved?'; and 'How, prior to the "epoch of revolutions", and if at all, is it possible for a member of the working class or anyone else for that matter to escape from their false consciousness and understand the true nature of their position?'

Lukacs: a philosophical reflex

By the 1920s and after several intense economic and political crises in the more advanced capitalist societies, it had become clear to some second-generation Marxist theorists that there would be no automatic transformation of proletarian consciousness. This forced them to attend to the two unanswered questions. The first of this new generation of theorists was Georg Lukacs, a Hungarian who was a neo-Kantian philosopher and member of Weber's circle before he became a Marxist and revolutionary. In general terms, Lukacs sought to fill the gaps in the otherwise realist Marxist tradition by deploying a set of ideas derived from the interpretivist tradition. More particularly, he sought to fill the gaps that had left the unanswered questions by mobilizing the interpretivists' belief that, unlike the other aspects of nature, society was internal as well as external to us, and so both depends on us thinking about it for its existence and does not so depend. On this basis, Lukacs brought two more specific ideas from the interpretivist tradition to his Marxism. First, the belief that there need be no sense of separation between individuals and society, because in the end society is nothing other than interactions between individuals. And second, the related but more specifically Weberian view that class position does not mean much to people unless they can connect that position with their daily lives, with their life chances. How Lukacs articulated these ideas with Marxist theory and used them to fill in the gaps in the latter was as follows: the sense of separation between individuals and society was unnatural (an idea shared but understood differently by interpretivists and Marxists); this unnatural condition was a product of the alienation or separation of some people from property in the means of production and the consequent division of people into classes (a Marxist idea); thus, if they wished to correct this condition, people had to realize how their class positions affected their lives (an interpretivist idea); this they could do by reflecting on their subjective experience (an interpretivist idea), helped by a revolutionary party (a Marxist/Leninist idea).

In short, Lukacs responded to the discovery of the gaps in Marxist theory by innovating at the level of the latter's ontological assumptions and drawing out the processual consequences (see Figure 6.1). The theoretical consequence of this shift, as set out in his 1924 essay *History and Class Consciousness*, was dramatic. Dramatic in that this innovation transformed the significance of commodity fetishism in the sense that it became a source of revolutionary hope instead of despair:

> In every aspect of daily life in which the individual worker imagines himself to be the subject of his own life he finds this to be an illusion that is destroyed by the immediacy of his existence. This forces upon him the knowledge that the most elementary gratification of his needs … forms therefore an aspect of the production and reproduction of capital … (Marx). The quantification of objects, their subordination to abstract mental categories makes its appearance in the life of the worker immediately as a process of abstraction of which he is the victim, and which cuts him off from his labor-power, forcing him to sell it on the market as a commodity, belonging to him. And by selling this, his only commodity, he integrates it (and himself: for his commodity is inseparable from his physical existence) into a specialized process that has been rationalized and mechanized, a process that he discovers already existing, complete and able to function without him and in which he is no more than a cipher reduced to an abstract quantity, a mechanized and rationalized tool.
>
> (Lukacs 1968:165–6)

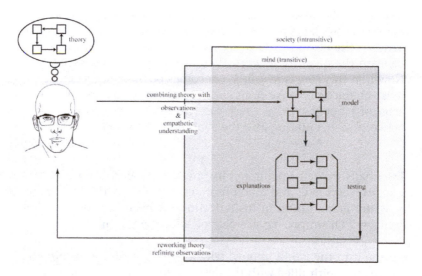

Figure 6.1 Lukacs and the synthesizing of interpretivism with realism

Contrary to the impression Lukacs seeks to give, the result of the turning of people into things ('reification' is Lukac's term) is the opposite of what might be expected on the basis of reading the later Marx:

[since] for the worker the reified character of the immediate manifestations of capitalist society receives the most extreme definition
possible. He is therefore forced into becoming the object of the
process by which he is turned into a commodity and reduced to a
mere quantity. But this very fact *forces him to surpass the immediacy
of his condition*. For as Marx says, 'Time is the place of human development'.

(Lukacs 1968: 166, emphasis added)

For Lukacs, then, and in a way that is closer to Hegel than to Marx,
reification spontaneously creates the possibility of de-reification, since
human beings almost automatically grasp the inherently exploitative character of capitalist society because they always know that they are not
things:

... when the worker knows himself as a commodity his knowledge
is practical. That is to say, this knowledge brings about an objective
structural change in the object of knowledge. In this consciousness
and through it the special objective character of labor as a commodity, its 'use-value' is submerged without a trace in the quantitative exchange categories of capitalism, now awakens and
becomes social reality. The special nature of labor as a commodity
now objectifies itself by means of this consciousness. The specific
nature of this kind of commodity had consisted in the fact that
beneath the cloak of the thing lay a relation between men, that
beneath the quantifying crust there was a qualitative, living core.
Now that this core is revealed it becomes possible to recognize the
fetish character of every commodity based on the commodity character of labor power: in every case we find its core, the relation
between men, entering into the evolution of society.

(Lukacs 1968: 169)

Essentially the same point, but inspired by rather different sources, was
made many years later and much more graphically by the great anti-colo-
nialist writer Franz Fanon in his reflection on hearing comments such as
'Dirty nigger!' Or simply, 'Look a Negro!' addressed to him:

I came into the world imbued with the will to find a meaning in
things, my spirit filled with the desire to attain to the source of the
world, and then I found that I was an object in the midst of other
objects. Sealed into that crushing objecthood, I turned beseech-
ingly to others. Their attention was a liberation, running over my
body suddenly abraded into nonbeing, endowing me once more
with an agility that I had thought lost, and by taking me out of the

world, restoring me to it. But just as I reached the other side, I stumbled, and the movements, the attitudes, the glances of the other fixed me there, in the sense in which a chemical solution is fixed by a dye. I was indignant; I demanded an explanation. Nothing happened. I burst apart. Now the fragments have been put together again by another self.

(Fanon 1967: 109)

Lukacs, having made his point about the inherent resistance of human beings to being treated as things, moves on to think about how what he calls this 'psychological consciousness' might be turned into class conciousness:

In addition to the mere contradiction – the automatic product of capitalism – a new element is required: the consciousness of the proletariat must become deed. But as the mere contradiction is raised to a consciously dialectical contradiction, as the act of becoming conscious turns into *a point of transition in practice*, we see once more in greater concreteness the character of proletarian dialectics as we have often described it: namely, since consciousness here is not the knowledge of an opposed object but is the self-consciousness of the object, *the act of consciousness overthrows the objective form of its object.*

(Lukacs 1968: 178, emphasis added)

The key or the 'new element', then, is getting people to act, to engage in 'praxis' which, as he goes on to explain, is the role of the party. The party is the instrument through which members of the proletariat can be brought to realize how their class position affects their lives. It achieves this by turning an invisible psychological consciousness into visible political action and in the process creating a transformative, revolutionary class consciousness since the members of the proletariat can see the power of their thought in action.

In sum, Lukacs fills the gaps in Marxist theory and responds to the unanswered questions by turning the neo-Kantian belief in the inherent meaningfulness of human life into a spontaneous antidote to reification that simply needs to be reinforced by the actions of the party. However, an element of inconsistency was thereby brought into Marxist metatheory with respect to its ontology. This proved to be a problem not only because society is understood to be both internal and external to individual human beings but also because – bearing in mind that metatheoretical changes lead to changes in research outcomes in the sense of models and theories – the internal dimension of social life is understood to be largely impervious to, and indeed more fundamental than, the external dimension. Hence what turned out to be the sociologically implausible and ethically corrosive belief that the institution responsible for the transformation of the internal dimension, the party, would be sufficient to bring about the conditions necessary for the discovery of the truth. I say 'ethically corrosive' because, as the custodian of so vital a role, the party had to be protected at all costs, even if one of them was the endless and bloody deferral of the production and dissemination of such knowledge, including that produced by Lukacs himself who was for many years considered deeply suspect by the same party.

Gramsci: a sociological reflex

Around the same time as Lukacs was developing his philosophical answer to Marxism's unanswered questions, the Italian theorist Antonio Gramsci was developing another kind of answer, and in so doing providing what turned out to be a more productive example – theoretically, empirically and politically – of the effects of metatheoretical changes on research outcomes. Like Lukacs, Gramsci also drew inspiration from outside the Marxist tradition and concluded that the party had a critical role to play in the practical answering of the questions. However, he used such inspiration and arrived at this conclusion through a very different route. His inspiration was the idea, first voiced by the nineteenth-century German linguist Wilhelm von Humbolt and later developed by the Italian idealist philosopher Benadetto Croce, that language was not simply a tool for the communication of thoughts that originated outside of itself, whether in the human mind or society but a source of meaning in itself (Seuren 1998). Thus the framework within which Gramsci approached the unanswered Marxist questions was one that required him to allow some autonomy to the linguistic and therefore the wider cultural realm and so suggested to him that the struggle for revolutionary consciousness had to be waged at the cultural as well as the economic and political levels. Gramsci used this idea not to complicate Marxism's ontology but instead to complicate its model of society; that is, he did not seek to fill the gap in Marxist theory by innovating philosophically but by innovating sociologically.

This sociological innovation was achieved through the elaboration of a set of three main concepts: 'civil society', 'hegemony', and 'historical bloc'. What Gramsci means by civil society is all those institutions that we commonly think of as non-state and non-political: families, churches, companies, trade unions, employers organizations, and voluntary associations of all kinds. He uses the concept of hegemony to explain how, in fact, classes rule through and therefore politicize these supposedly private institutions:

> I have remarked elsewhere that in any given society nobody is disorganized and without party, provided that one takes organization

and party in a broad and not a formal sense. In this multiplicity of private associations (which are of two kinds: natural, and contractual or voluntary) one or more predominates relatively or absolutely – constituting the hegemonic apparatus of one social group over the rest of the population (or civil society): the basis for the State in the narrow sense of the governmental-coercive apparatus. It always happens that individuals belong to more than one private association, and often to associations which are objectively in contradiction to one another.

(Gramsci 1971: 264–5)

Thus, in Gramsci's view, people come to accept their positions in cap-italist society not simply because they participate in buying and selling, but also because they participate in many other activities that do not call into question the structure of capitalist society with the result that they come to share certain common-sense understandings that immunize them, so to speak, against any questioning. The consequence is that societies are ruled not by single classes but by historical blocs (class alliances), within which the subordinate classes have the illusion of organizing themselves and pursuing their own objectives. In sum, Gramsci responds to Marxism's unanswered questions and fills in the gaps in its theory by insisting on the importance of a hitherto neglected realm *within* the social rather than other to it, namely that of language and those social things that live in it that are known collectively as 'culture'. Accordingly, the conception of the party derived from Gramsci's work and gradually developed in Italy after 1945 was far more inclusive and pluralistic than the Leninist conception to which Lukacs remained loyal – the party was conceived of more as a community interacting with its wider social environment and allowing new, if not disinterested, thought than as a specialized instrument for the seizure of power on the basis of a predetemined truth.

From a structuralist to an archaeological reflex

Lukacs had a direct influence on the approaches to the power/knowledge issue taken by the Frankfurt School and the critical theory that grew out of it, including in the, to me, unfortunate sense that these two bodies of theory continued to address the issue abstractly and metatheoretically rather than substantively and sociologically. Gramsci's work, especially the concept of hegemony, was rediscovered in the 1960s and later articulated with what became known as post-structuralism. The critical intermediary here was the structuralist Marxist Louis Althusser who, inspired also by Mao Tse Tung's (1966) ideas concerning the relations between what Mao termed 'primary' (economic) and 'secondary' (political, ideological) contradictions, reformulated many of Gramsci's ideas within an overall framework that mod-elled societies as dynamic 'social formations' governed by a complex 'struc-tural causality' that allowed for both the reinforcement and undermining of the structures of domination (Benton 1984; Lopez 2003). Within this frame-work, Althusser (1971) reconceptualized Gramsci's hegemonic relations as 'ideological state apparatuses'. Unfortunately, much of the analytical subtlety allowed by Gramsci's original formulation was lost in the process. However, the way in which Althusser explained how these apparatuses worked repre-sented a definite advance in that it addressed an issue that Gramsci had not addressed. Inspired in this aspect of his work by Sigmund Freud and his 'rene-gade' follower Jacques Lacan, but also in a very similar way to Durkheim (see above, pp. 46–54), Althusser pictured this process as one of 'hailing' or 'interpellation':

> I shall then suggest that ideology 'acts' or 'functions' in such a way that it 'recruits' subjects among the individuals (it recruits them all), or 'transforms' the individuals into subjects (it transforms them all) by that very precise operation which I have called interpellation or hailing, and which can be imagined along the lines of the most commonplace everyday police (or other) hailing: 'Hey, you there!' Assuming that the theoretical scene I have imagined takes place in the street, the hailed individual will turn round. By this mere one-hundred-and-eighty-degree physical conversion, he becomes a subject. Why? Because he has recognized that the hail was 'really' addressed to him, and that 'it was really him who was hailed' (and not someone else). Experience shows that, the practical telecommu-nication of hailings is such that they hardly ever miss their man: verbal call or whistle, the one hailed always recognizes that it is really him who is being hailed. And yet it is a strange phenomenon, and one which cannot be explained solely by 'guilt feelings', despite the large numbers who 'have something on their consciences'. Naturally for the convenience and clarity of my little theoretical theatre I have had to present things in the form of a sequence, with a before and an after, and thus in the form of a temporal succession. There are individuals walking along. Somewhere (usually behind them) the hail rings out 'Hey, you there!' One individual (nine times out of ten it is the right one) turns round, believing/suspecting/knowing that it is for him, i.e. recognizing that 'it really is he' who is meant by the hailing. But in reality these things happen without any succession. The existence of ideology and the hailing or inter-pellation of individuals as subjects are one and the same thing.
>
> I might add: what thus seems to take place outside ideology (to be precise, in the street), in reality takes place in ideology.
>
> (Althusser 1971: 162–3)

The point of connection between the concept of interpellation and the power/knowledge issue is that the subject positions about which Althusser talks become part of our individual identities, part of who we think we are. Thus, if someone addresses us in terms of one or other of these elements of our 'identities', they are probably more than half way to getting us to do their bidding because we already think of ourselves as people who should do whatever it is we are being asked to do – that is, be 'good children', 'good students', 'good citizens', 'good sociologists', or whatever. Thus the interactions critical to everyday understandings of the social world occur, not 'in the street' at the moment of hailing as Fanon suggested, nor indeed in the factory, as Lukacs suggested, but have already occurred in the course of our induction into language and social life more generally. But where do these subject positions and the expectations they carry with them come from and why do they gain their power over us? This is the question that Foucault answered so influentially and which is critical to the development of the realist reflexivity I am seeking to develop.[1] However, before outlining Foucault's answer, I will first briefly summarize Ferdinand de Saussure's theory of language because this went far beyond von Humbolt and Croce's work in rethinking the nature of language, and in my view, is what made it possible for Foucault to provide us with the means to locate ourselves for reflexive purposes within the worlds of knowledge *and* power simultaneously.

Saussure's linguistic revolution began with the rejection of the search for origins and the consequent vision dependency that had dominated linguistics for much of its history. Instead, and in contrast to the early Wittgenstein, Saussure, who was directly inspired by Durkheim's understanding of the *sui generis* nature of social facts, proposed that language should not be thought of in a representationalist manner as originating in a human naming process but as simply an intrinsic property of the social relations that make speech possible and which therefore have always affected what we see. For Saussure, this time in contrast to the later Wittgenstein, language's critical components are those that make it possible (*langue*) rather than those that give it expression (parole), and those that account for its stability (synchronic relations) rather than for its transformation (diachronic relations). In order to describe the core of *langue's* synchronic relations, Saussure revived the ancient Stoic vocabulary for analysing language and spoke of it as comprising 'signifiers' (sets of sound differences or impressions) and 'signifieds' (sets of mental or conceptual differences or impressions). These are given value or meaning through being brought into alignment with one another to form signs (words) by the operation of syntagmatic relations (the rules of syntax, for example) and associative or paradigmatic relations (lexicons).

Saussure's transformation of our understanding of language has three consequences both for how human beings locate themselves in society and for theoretical activity. First, possessed of the inner motor, so to speak, described in the preceding paragraph and therefore governed by a specific ecology, language and the cultural or discursive things that exist within it possess an irreducible if necessarily incomplete autonomy that makes them permanently capable of escaping from the control of both subjects and other social processes. Because of this autonomy a tiny sphere of both freedom and danger is available to human beings in general and social scientists in particular in that it is this autonomy that imposes a reflexive responsibility on us to ask if any social identities we adopt are ethically defensible or, in the case of social scientists, if the concepts we use are the product of sociological reasoning rather than the 'unthought'. Second, not only are the connections between signifiers and signifieds arbitrary in the sense that neither determines what the other must be, but therefore the relationship between signs and the things and actions in the world to which they refer must therefore be arbitrary too. That is, a word including a theoretical term cannot exist on its own and as a meaningful entity as a picture or representation of the world. Instead it can only exist as an element in a much larger system of picturing or representing the world, of giving it meaning that as such is at least partially governed by processes and mechanisms intrinsic to itself which owe nothing to the world external to it.

However, third, because of the arbitrariness of the relations between signs and their extra-linguistic referents, an understanding of *langue* alone cannot tell us why its users in fact take words to refer to certain specific things and actions in the world and not simply certain ideas or descriptions of them. In Saussure's own and seldom-noticed words:

> ... the arbitrariness of language radically separates it from all other institutions. This is apparent from the way in which language evolves. Nothing could be more complex. As it is a product of both the social force and time, no one can change anything in it, and on the other hand, the arbitrariness of its signs theoretically entails the freedom of establishing just any relationship between phonetic substance and ideas. The result is that each of the two elements united in a sign maintains its own life to a degree unknown elsewhere, and that language changes, or rather evolves, under the influence of all the forces which can effect either sounds or meanings. The evolution is inevitable; there is no example of a single language that resists it. After a certain period of time, some obvious shifts can always be recorded.
>
> (Saussure 1974: 76)

Thus to understand linguistic change and therefore by extension to understand linguistic and theoretical reference requires much more than an understanding of the structures and processes intrinsic to *langue*. What this 'much more' involves, the imbrication of language with social life in general to form visualities, will be discussed at length below, when I outline Foucault's concept of 'discursive formation', as will the reflexive method-ological freedom and consequent responsibility that is granted to and imposed upon the social scientist by language's incomplete autonomy and consequent location in the field of power.

In the simplest sense, the carriers of this 'much more' are not the individuals to whom the social constructionists urge us to listen, but what Foucault refers to as discourses or the more-or-less formal sets of interlinked concepts, whether in the form of religions, ideologies, sciences or whatever, that organize, order and constrain our thought and so establish and secure certain 'regimes of truth'. As such this is a rather familiar even common-sensical idea. However, what makes Foucault's deployment of it far from commonsensical is that he not only understands that discourses do not achieve their effects by logic alone, but he also finds a way to investigate the nature of the additional factors involved. Foucault summarizes the differences between his position and those that preceded it by saying that, whereas his predecessors had conceptualized their textual evidence as 'documents' in which the voices of their authors and those they referred to could be heard, he conceptualizes such evidence as 'monuments' that can only be understood by uncovering their surroundings – that is, archaeolog-ically. And, as elaborated in his *Archaeology of Knowledge* of 1972, what is found when these surroundings are uncovered are what he refers to as 'discursive formations' and their 'rules of formation' (see Figure 6.2).

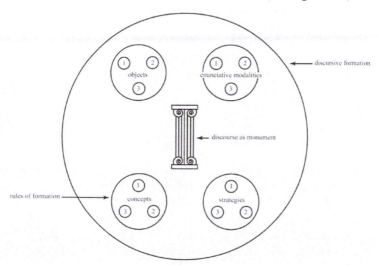

Figure 6.2 The discursive formation and its rules of formation

The questions that Foucault addresses with the latter two concepts are: 1) How do discourses develop? 2) How do they come to be taken as comprising authoritative and therefore to some degree socially determinant statements about the nature of the world? His answer to these questions is that discourses develop and gain their determinative power as a consequence of the largely unwilled interaction between four elements: *objects* (the things they are about); *enunciative modalities* (the ways these things are spoken of); *concepts* (the intellectual constructs that are used to speak about them); and *strategies* (the ways in which these constructs are combined or thematized). What determines the nature and power effects of the interactions between these elements are their respective rules or, better, the factors that continuously determine their formation and re-formation.

In the case of *objects* these factors, partially translated from Foucault's rather fearsome terminology, are:

1   the institutional sites wherein the objects of interest are problematized and so become socially visible – for example, the Catholic confessional in the case of psychiatry, the marketplace in the case of economics, and the court in the case of law;
2   the appearance or presence of authorities of delimitation – experts and latterly professionals of all kinds – who possess the power to decide what is or is not an instance of the object of interest;
3   the production or presence of a grid of specification produced by these experts which delimits the object of interest and distinguishes it from other objects – examples include general concepts such as the body, the economy, the polity, society, and the law.

Concerning *enunciative modalities* or ways of making statements, these factors are:

1   the credentials of the qualified speakers;
2   the institutional sites from whence they speak;
3   the modes of interrogation they engage in (listening, questioning, or looking, for example).

With respect to *concepts*, these factors are:

1   their order and forms of succession or emergence and development;
2   their fields and forms of coexistence or the general methodologies that are used to determine their legitimacy as instances of knowledge;
3   the procedures for intervention or the ways of working within the conceptual field as exemplified by rewriting, transcribing, and translating.

Finally, with regard to *strategies* these factors are:

1   the identities, similarities, differences, and combinations of such strategies;
2   the identification of thematic authorities, whether these are located within the field of discourse involved or external to it and are therefore authorities by analogy;
3   the identification of the *'function'* that the discourse under study must carry out *'in a field of non-discursive practices'* such as the economic and political realms, and *'possible positions of desire in relation to discourse'*.

(Foucault 1972: 68)

In sum, and in addition to explaining why science so often fails to speak truth to power, Foucault provides a means for both picturing the highly complex concatenations of discursive and non-discursive elements that produce such instances of power/knowledge as social theory, and explaining why such theories picture the social in the way they do.

Conclusion

If you wish both to be reflexive and to maintain a realist metatheoretical position, reflexivity should not be narrowly understood as simply as looking inward at your abstract assumptions, biases and, *à la* Derrida (1977), your prior reading. Of course all of these personal attributes are important and have powerful effects, but they do not mean that what we see and what we picture in our theories are simply artefacts of the interactive effects of these internal, mentalistic elements and influences alone. As realism insists, the external world must be of a certain character for us to be able to perceive it and interact with it as we do (experimentally, for example), no matter how various our perceptions may be and regardless of the fact that we will never know what the external world is really like for itself, so to speak. The critically important aspect of what the external world's character must be in the current context is that it is not only external to us but alive, that in particular, as Durkheim insisted, society as such is also alive and therefore in some sense 'telling' us what we are seeing and what we should think about it. The result is that 'the sociologist is saddled with the task of knowing an object – the social world – of which he is the product, in a way such that the problems that he raises about it and the concepts he uses have every chance of being the product of the object itself' (Bourdieu and Wacquant 1992: 235). Thus, 'for a sociologist more than any other thinker, to leave one's thought in a state of unthought is to condemn oneself to be nothing more than the *instrument* of that which one claims to think' (Bourdieu and Wacquant 1992: 238). Foucault's achievement, then, is to have completed for the time being the transformation of the insights contained in Hegel and Marx's thought concerning power's inability to face the truth as to its source into a visible and researchable process. In so doing, he has also provided social scientists with a way to reflect on the unthought and so preserve their chances of pursuing if not disinterested knowledge then at least a knowledge that is aware of its own historicity and fallibility.

Note

1   Elaborated justifications for reading Foucault as a realist may be found in Pearce and Woodiwiss (2001); Woodiwiss (2001): 147–61.

7   Atlanticism and the inward turn

*Cultural imperialism rests on the power to universalize
particularisms linked to a single historical tradition by causing
them to be misrecognized as such ... The neutralization of the
historical context resulting from the international circulation of
texts and the correlative forgetting of their originating historical
conditions produces an apparent universalization further abetted
by the further work of 'theorization.' A kind of fictional
axiomatization fit to produce the illusion of pure genesis ... tends
to obfuscate the historical roots of a whole ensemble of questions
and notions ... now tacitly constituted as model for every other
[society] and as yardstick for all things.*

(Bourdieu and Wacquant
'On the Cunning of Imperialist Reason')

In this chapter and that which follows, I will illustrate what a realist reflexivity involves and the sort of results it produces by using my realist reading
of Foucault's concept of a discursive formation in order both to explain how
Durkheim's sociological project was subverted during the second half of the
twentieth century and to contribute to the restoration of the knowledge
that was thereby forgotten. I will take as my focus the eclipse of the concept
of class by that of identity (a set of psychological and/or social attributes
shared by groups of individuals and distinguishing them from others) at the
core of sociological discourse. For me, four factors were critical in effecting
this eclipse (the replacement of one visualization of society by another),
and the discussion of them will take us deep into the structure of the discursive formation that governed the nature of the picturing machine that
was social theory in the late twentieth century, albeit in a highly schematic
way. First, within the context of the Cold War and the signing of the North
Atlantic Treaty of 1949, the institutional site wherein sociological thinking
developed became Atlantic rather than European in the sense that the

United States with its distinctively individualistic culture became the principal locus of sociology's development (on the development of Atlanticism more generally, see Van der Pijl 1997). Hence the narrowness of the nature of the 'common heritage and civilization' specified in the preamble to the North Atlantic Treaty:

> The Parties to this Treaty reaffirm their faith in the purposes and principles of the Charter of the United Nations and their desire to live in peace with all peoples and all governments. *They are determined to safeguard the freedom, common heritage and civilization of their peoples, founded on the principles of democracy, individual liberty and the rule of law.* They seek to promote stability and well-being in the North Atlantic area. They are resolved to unite their efforts for collective defence and for the preservation of peace and security. They therefore agree to this North Atlantic Treaty: ...

Note the absence of any mention of trade unions, social partnership, the welfare state, or of any other by then already distinctively Western European civilizational elements. Second, and relatedly, American sociology did not share the European interest in class as a major determinant and instantiation of social structure but instead was far more interested in the tensions between individuals and social order as demarcated by the terms modernity, race, ethnicity, gender and, ultimately, identity. Third, following the 'inward' turn that was part and parcel of the United States' unique entry into a condition of literal postmodernity in the late 1970s, the preeminence of such issues was reinforced by the rise of feminist and postmodernist critiques of what they termed 'malestream' or 'foundationalist' epistemologies respectively. The net result was that the concept of identity ultimately became central to the sociological picture of Europe, and especially Britain, too. Finally, and ironically, if you accept my realist reading of Foucault, one of the main instruments of this reinforcement was Foucault's concept of discourse.

I should make a number of things clear before providing a more detailed account of these differences, reinforcements and instruments, as well as their consequences. First, I will not be arguing that the rise of identity theory was intentionally sponsored in order to bring about a decline of interest in the concept of class. Nor will I be arguing that the rise of identity theory in itself explains this decline. Rather, what I will argue is that the decline of interest in class was a product of the changing character of the sociological unthought or discursive formation – that is, a largely unintended consequence of the affinity between the rise of a new form of identity theory and the occurrence of a wider set of conceptual and social developments of which that rise was a part. Second, mindful of my own obligation to be reflexive in the established sense, I should also acknowledge that, given my commitment to the Durkheimian project, I have long been sceptical of the sociological value of the concept of identity simply because it is an import from psychology. Thus, at most, it seems to me that it may play a role as a stimulating but temporary analogy in the absence of a properly sociological conceptualization of whatever it is that the concept of identity is being used to talk about (on the proper and improper use of analogies or metaphors in sociological work, see Lopez 2003). Moreover, my scepticism is only increased by the fact that the regions of psychology from whence the concept of identity was borrowed were such humanistic social psychologies as symbolic interactionism and that associated with cognitive psychology. This is because such social psychologies, especially in the postmodernist variant represented by Kenneth Gergen's *The Saturated Self* (2000) tend to dissolve the psychological and the sociological into one another (Craib 1998). In my view, the most general theory-related problem with such social psychologies is that they impose an overwhelming explanatory burden on an analogy because those who try to provide explanations on such a basis deny themselves many of the conceptual resources of the two disciplines (as additional examples of such self-denial, see the accounts of the 'social self' provided by Giddens 1991, and Jenkins 1996).

Finally, I should also say that I have never been convinced that an identity could be an attribute of, or could define, a group, whether ethnic, racial or whatever, in the sense that all group members share certain characteristics that also differentiate them from other groups. Such a conception would seem to repeat very precisely the problematic aspects to be specified below (see pp. 119–21) with respect to the traditional conceptions of the classes that these supposed identities have replaced; that is, their explanatory worth may also be readily called into question if all of the traits and consequent behaviour patterns ascribed to the supposed identities are not found to be present amongst all of their supposed bearers. For example, how many elements of the supposed gay identity does it take to make a person gay? Is a sexual preference for people of one's own sex sufficient? My sense of the literature is that the answer is 'no' since such a position would be regarded as 'essentialist', and that such a person should instead be regarded as simply a man who has sex with men. However, there is no equally clear answer as to which or how many other elements are required to qualify someone as a gay person. Nor is it at all clear what if anything could follow from the 'possession' of so labile an identity with respect to a person's actions in other areas of social life such as politics or even consumption. For all these reasons, then, it seems to me that what needs explaining is not only why identity groups became so important in the late twentieth-century global north but also why the concept of identity became so influential (to the degree that it contributed greatly to the development of such groups). Thus there is definitely something to study around the rise of identity groups but it is as much about why the concept was so readily available and why it was taken up so widely as about why the groups so defined became so socially prominent.

From capitalism to modernity

In order to appreciate the specificity of a discursive formation at a particular point in time, it is helpful to compare it with its state at another point in time. Consequently, I will try to bring out the distinctiveness of the state of the discursive formation pertaining to sociology as a whole in the 1990s by comparing it with its state in the 1930s. In the 1930s, sociology was still primarily a European and even country-specific area of intellectual activity within which efforts at synthesis and writing textbooks were few and far between. The two leading national traditions were those of France (Marxist and Durkheimian) and Germany (Marxist and Weberian). The lesser traditions such as those of Britain and the United States were for complex reasons (Abrams 1968; Bannister 1991; Anderson 1992; Turner 1994) less theory-driven and much more empirically and policy oriented. Nonetheless, it is clear that, even in the latter two countries, the social-structural/institutional complex within which the discipline was emerging was seen as that which the classical theorists wrote about, namely that formed by the nexus of the state, the capitalist economy and liberal-democratic governmental discourses of rule. Thus Marx, Weber and Durkheim became the principal authorities defining the field with the result that the central object of interest to the discipline was demarcated and pictured as something called capitalism, which, in turn, and to varying degrees, was understood to be animated by class tensions and conflicts. Accordingly, the vocabularies produced by these classical theorists defined much of the expert language that had to be used if someone wished to be taken seriously when speaking about social life. Similarly, these theorists also provided much of the discipline's conceptual infrastructure, whilst the differences between them, especially at the metatheoretical level, stimulated the production of different strategic or overall theorizations. This, then, was the conjuncture with respect to sociology's discursive formation that produced what we now refer to as classical sociology. However, as Saussure intimated (see above, pp. 99–101) and in ways that Foucault made explicit, discursive formations and the complex optical mechanisms that they produce are always changing since the rules of formation are always operating with the result that no conjuncture holds for long. Indeed particular discourses (different schools of social theory, for example) commonly survive only by being constantly reinvented even when they are not data-driven.

Fittingly, what turned out to be the first significant postclassical school of non-Marxist social theory was initiated in the United States rather than Europe but by an American who had studied in Germany, Talcott Parsons.

In his *Structure of Social Action* (1937), Parsons produced a distinctively American reading of what he was largely responsible for isolating as classical sociology. It was distinctively American in the sense that classical theory was read not as picturing the structure of capitalist society but, on the contrary, as contributing critical elements to the construction of a new set of lenses in the form of precisely the kind of creative individualistic theory that had for Durkheim 'radically prevented the establishment of sociology', namely the 'voluntaristic theory of action'. Thereafter social theory developed in an intellectually as well as geopolitically Atlanticist institutional context within which the American side gradually became predominant. This said, there was a period – from the late 1940s to the mid-1960s – during which American social theory in general and Parsons' theory more particularly transformed itself into an apparently European-style holistic theory. This theory, however, was only apparently sociologistic because, despite the predominance of the established empiricist tradition in the United States (see above, pp. 25–30), it was produced not so much by empirically grounded theoretical reason as by Parsons, very likely stimulated by his wartime investigations of the social structures of Germany and Japan (Parsons 1997), turning his remarkable mind away from the theory of creative individualism and towards the specifically American social conditions that he thought had facilitated the production of the theory, and rationalistically developing an abstract language to describe these conditions. Soon afterwards others gave the label 'modernity' to the abstract representation that Parsons had projected onto the United States (see Figure 7.1).

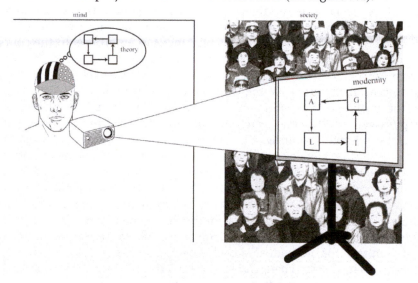

Figure 7.1 Parsons and the projection of social theory onto society

Why 'modernity'? Startlingly, and with consequences that are discussed at length elsewhere (Woodiwiss 1990b: Chapter 7; 1997; 2001:
Chapter 3), few of those who, whether in the United States or Europe, took
it up so readily in the 1980s inquired into the sociological genealogy of the
term modernity when it rather surprisingly resurfaced as an after-effect of
the rise of postmodernism; and certainly no one inquired into the developing discursive formation that accounted for its availability as a key
element in contemporary theoretical discourse. Rather, those who took up
the concept defined it as they wished, or so they thought. Thus they
defined it, depending on the context, by identifying it with the emergence
of Cartesian epistemology, the occurrence of the first and/or second industrial revolutions, or with the appearance of a creative, self-reflexive individualism. In so doing they failed to realize that this selection or, as
Foucault would put it, 'dispersion' of factors precisely, if incompletely, repli-
cated the unthought or discursive formation of Atlanticist social theory, as
I will now show.

It is commonly agreed that the discourse of modernism emerged as an
aspect of a broad and therefore very loosely defined movement within the
arts, which was indeed informed and affected by all of the developments
just mentioned. In the course of its emergence, the initially negative con-
notations of the word 'modern' were gradually reversed as modernism
slowly gestated during the nineteenth century, became widely visible
around the turn of the century in the English-speaking world, belatedly
became conscious of itself as 'modernism' during the 1930s (Bradbury and
McFarlane 1991). What is far less commonly recognized is that the expansion of the meaning of 'modernity' to include a social rather than simply
an aesthetic condition was primarily an American enterprise. In the course
of the 1940s, and thanks in large measure to intellectual emigres from
fascist Europe, the United States became the centre of modernist experi-
mentation in the arts (*vide* the displacement of Paris by New York as the
artistic capital of the world with the rise of Abstract Expressionism –
http://www.artcyclopedia, search in 'Movements' – as the first major post-
surrealist school of painting). Consequently, a stoical, world-weary reading
of the otherwise generally critical and progressive social diagnosis implicit
in aesthetic modernism took hold of certain sections of the United States'
cultural intelligensia. This was a reading to the effect that, qualified only by
the existence of the New Deal or 'social modernist' (Woodiwiss 1993:
Chapter 1) package of reforms (a minimalist welfare state, the licensing
of responsible trade unions, and a societal commitment to increased
opportunities for individual advancement), knowing self-reflexiveness,
competitiveness and changefulness were all that could or should be
expected in or of the modern world – to want more risked the return of
concentration camps. As the 1940s came to a close and the Cold War
commenced, this was a diagnosis that provided a new analytical vocabu-

lary, and therefore a convenient resting place, for such soon to be highly influential sociologists as Daniel Bell and David Riesman on their journeys from 'socialist estrangement' to 'reconciliation' with the American status-quo – journeys that they justified as having been made necessary by American socialism's failure to measure up to the demands of what they termed 'modernity' (Bell 1967: 5; Brick 1986, passim; Gilman 2004; Wolfe 1988: 66–8; Woodiwiss 1990b: Chapter 7 and 1993).

Talcott Parsons: systematizing the American dream

During the 1950s Parsons was gradually recognized as *the* theorist of the United State's newly claimed modernity. His first book, the *Structure of Social Action* (1937), had both defined what had already come to be regarded as the core concerns of postwar sociological theory and identified the key contributors. Significantly, these concerns excluded capitalism as such, and Parsons' list of key theorists emphasized the importance of Durkheim and Weber while it minimized that of Marx. As an individualist living in a very individualistic society, it seemed obvious to Parsons that the most basic social problem was not alienation or the manufactured inability of most people to survive on the basis of their own resources, as had been the case for Marx, but what Parsons terms the 'problem of order'. Inspired by another of the seventeenth-century political philosophers anathematized by Durkheim, Thomas Hobbes, Parsons defined the project of sociology as understanding how societies are generally orderly rather than chaotic, despite being aggregates of intrinsically competitive individuals. What interested him in the work of Durkheim and Weber was what he regarded as their shared convergence on a 'voluntaristic theory of action'. This is the sociological equivalent of Adam's Smith's conception of the competitive economy as ordered by the 'hidden hand' of the market in that it centres on the apparently equally paradoxical idea that the voluntary actions of individuals produce another 'hidden hand', one that ensures that these actions are mutually beneficial, namely a set of shared values.

More specifically, Parsons argues that the fundamental building block of society and therefore of sociology too is the 'unit act', which is a single action pictured as comprising the following components: an end, some means, some constraining conditions, and a set of values that are used to decide the choice of goals and means. Given this specification of the core element of what might appropriately be termed the atomic structure of social life, the task before sociological theory is a clear if not an easy one: to explain how these unit acts come to form a coherent whole. The answer Parsons later provided to this question had two parts. First, within any particular society or nation state a common or shared set of values always already holds sway. Second, the central purpose of the most important institutions in any society is to ensure that its members accept and act upon these values.

Before elaborating on these points, I would like to step back for a moment and point out that the idea behind the unit act – namely that the voluntary actions of individuals are ordered by shared values – has already been encountered in this text, specifically in the accounts provided earlier of the fetishism of commodities and hegemony. The surprising difference between the Parsonian and Marxist formulations of this idea is that whereas Parsons the individualist embraced the paradox involved, the Marxists refused it because they regarded it as requiring the continued stunting of individuality!

Returning to Parsons, as he prepared what was to become his magnum opus, *The Social System* (1951), he engaged in a set of intensive discussions with scholars from other social science disciplines, notably psychology and anthropology (Parsons and Shils 1951). These discussions convinced him that although it was possible to distinguish the social system from the personality and cultural systems, it was not possible to separate these systems from one another analytically, let alone empirically. This was because, confirming the thought that informs the specification of the unit act, the job of the social system was precisely to integrate the personality and cultural systems (see Figure 7.2). In *The Social System* itself Parsons specifies the key concepts necessary to picture how this integrative task is accomplished as 'status' (for Parsons as opposed to Weber, simply a position in an institution) and 'role' (the performance of a status). Provided that a system of status/roles is not incompatible with the basic needs of individuals as defined by the personality system nor does it invoke values that are unacceptable to a significant

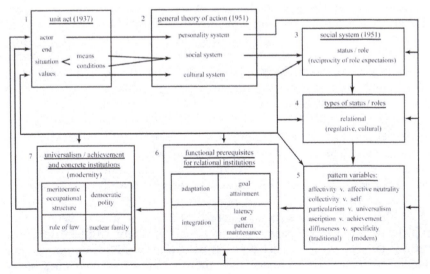

Figure 7.2 Key moments in the development and structure of Parsonian theory

segment of the society, the end result should be the securing of a 'reciprocity of role expectations' (Parsons 1951: 42) in that all actors should act as others expect them to act, across the whole range of status/roles and whether the latter are regulative or cultural. The 'reciprocity of role expectations' is therefore dubbed by Parsons the 'fundamental theorem of sociology'.

Parsons recognizes, of course, that social systems vary and allows for this through his elaboration of a set of 'pattern variables' which he presents as a trans-historical set of the value dilemmas faced by actors as they 'orient' themselves to the performance of their statuses. Abstractly, then, social actors face a set of five choices as to the nature of the values that will guide their role performance:

- Affectivity versus affective neutrality (will they act on the basis of emotion or not?).
- Collectivity orientation versus self-orientation (will they act in the interests of the collectivity or themselves?).
- Particularism versus universalism (will they act differently or in the same way towards others?).
- Ascription versus achievement (will they relate to others on the basis of who the others are or on the basis of what the others have achieved?).
- Diffuseness versus specificity (will they relate to others across a wide or a restricted range of activities?).

In reality, however, these choices have always already been predecided for any society by the values that have become established within it. The set comprising the first term in each pair quickly came to be regarded as characterizing traditional societies, and the set comprising the second term in each pair was taken as characterizing modern societies. Equally quickly, technological development was identified as the main driving force of modernization. Thus the ways in which actors should respond to what, in order to save time rather than because he was a committed functionalist, Parsons (1951: Chapter 5) specifies as the four fundamental needs of a social system are also predecided. These four fundamental needs or 'functional prerequisites' are, as summarized in what has become known as Parsons' AGIL model: adaptation (met through the organization of work); goal attainment (met through the polity); integration (met through legal and other regulatory institutions); and pattern maintenance or latency (met through the family and other stress management institutions). Uniquely in Parsons' view, and because he considered it to be the most technologically advanced society, the values that determine the particular way in which these needs are met by actors in the United States are rooted in the modern solutions to the dilemmas represented in the pattern variable schema. And what this means therefore is that in a modern society, guided by the values of universalism and achievement, the reciprocity of role expectations is assured because the adaptation need is met through a meritocratic occupational structure, the goal attainment need is met through a democratic polity, the integrative need is met through the rule of law, and the pattern maintenance need is met through the nuclear family.

Putting to one side any doubts one might reasonably have about the accuracy of such a characterization of the nature of American society, this was how, sociologically, the United States came to regard itself as the quintessentially modern society and gained its self-appointed global mission:

> The work of modernization is the burden of this age. It is our rock. It is an objective that is not confined to a single place or region, to a particular country or class, or to a privileged group of people.
>
> Modernization is a special kind of hope. Embodied in it are all the past revolutions of history and all the supreme human desires. The modernization revolution is epic in its scale and moral in its significance. Its consequences may be frightening. Any goal that is so desperately desired creates political power, and this force may not always be used wisely or well. Whatever direction it may take, the struggle to modernize is what has given meaning to our generation. It tests our cherished institutions and our beliefs.
>
> It puts our country in the market place of ideas and ideologies. So compelling a force has it become that we are forced to ask new questions of our own institutions. Each country, whether modernized or modernizing stands in both judgment and fear of the results. Our own society is no exception.
>
> (Apter 1965: 1–2)

In sum, the genealogy of modernity as a sociological term begins with the United States' hegemonic, individualistic ideology being aestheticized because of that country's position as a haven for modernistically inclined artists and intellectuals before being, second, transformed into an apparently holistic sociology, and third, transformed back into an ideology that, of course, contained a denial that it was any such thing. In the course of these transformations, the world weariness of the 1940s became the celebratory discourse of the late 1950s and early 1960s. For Bell *et al.* the major cause for celebration and, simultaneously, the mechanism of denial was a claim that both reflected the technologically advanced nature of American society and summarized all the developments that had supposedly made the United States the archetypal modern society – namely the claim that the United States had witnessed the 'end of ideology' (Bell 1960) or the displacement of ideology by science as the guiding discourse of social development. Hence, then, the continuing sociological appeal of native American empiricism and its unlikely coupling with Parsons' rationalistic structural functionalism to create the 'middle-range' theory that became the American way of theory (see above, pp. 25–30).

The decline of modernity and the rise of identity

When some 30 or so years later and in the aftermath of postmodernism (see below, pp. 130–6) some Western European social scientists enthusiastically imported the concept of modernity into their discourse, their picture of their own societies did not change because they accepted either the American empiricist project or its unlikely partner. They did not. Rather, their picture of European societies changed because they belatedly accepted the language of Parsonianism and modernization theory and thereby unknowingly bought into the Atlanticist unthought and accepted the humanistic ontology that underpinned these two bodies of theory (Woodiwiss 2001: Chapter 2). In the United States this humanistic ontology and its symptomatic individualism had returned to the foreground when the appearance of social consensus fostered by the image of America as *the* modern society was shattered by the economic weakness and conflicts that marked the late 1960s and early 1970s. For American sociologists like Bell (1976) the resulting social turmoil simply confirmed the United States' advanced modernity because it reflected the stresses and strains associated with the increasing size of the middle class (Bell 1973): 'the classic trajectory of expectations … tells us that no society that promises justice and … slowly begins to open the way, can then expect to ride out the consequent whirlwind in a comfortable fashion' (Bell 1976: 179). An alternative view, confirmed by subsequent developments (Sandage 2005) is that these were years during which the United States' claim to have attained a state of advanced modernity began to look rather hollow, because this was a period of considerable class tension, as indicated by the high levels of official and unofficial employee actions in the industrial sector of the economy and increasing inequality, as it also saw the beginning of a successful and still ongoing effort to reduce the perquisites of the middle class with the result that, although the middle class grew larger, all but its upper echelon became relatively poorer (Woodiwiss 1993: Part 2). In addition, unhappiness about the war in Vietnam interacted with these class tensions and a related set of intergenerational tensions to produce a whole raft of initially youth-oriented, middle-class social movements pursuing such goals as women's liberation, gay liberation, and 'participatory democracy'. However, as will become apparent below, the emergence of what was called at the time the 'Movement' did not mean that the influence of Parsons' theory and of the intellectual and social forces that produced it came to an end – far from it.

By the mid-1970s, the economy was on the upturn, and relatedly the labour force was quiescent, the war had ended, and order had been more-or-less restored to the streets except for what proved to be an intensifying battle between 'police and thieves':

> By all accounts, students entering higher education in the mid-1970s became much more vocationally oriented ... More notice-ably, the already employed, the future 'yuppies', began to seek meaning in the diffused and commercialized development of Movement themes: greater drug use, but for the sake of the 'sharp-ness' that comes from cocaine rather than the 'mind expansion' associated with marijuana and LSD; self-awareness, but through commodified and individualized therapies rather than 'tribal' rituals; feminism, but through the pursuit of a pragmatic Equal Rights Amendment rather than a romantic 'liberation'; civic activism, but in the cause of ecology rather than civil rights; in sum, a 'new age' rather than a 'revolution' was sought.
>
> (Woodiwiss 1993: 97)

The return of relative tranquility saw not only an inward turn on the part of many disappointed as well as reconciled social groups and individ-uals but also the beginning of the withdrawal of the state from its role as the ultimate guarantor of the values, policies and programmes – principally those associated with the broadening equalization of opportunities – that had hitherto confirmed the United States' status as *the* modern society for many of its citizens. As a result, the United States became the first, and probably the only, literally postmodern society – no other society's dis-course of rule had used the term 'modern' to define itself or so clearly equated its claim to modernity with opportunity for all. However, even those self-described conservatives who had consciously rejected the social modernism of the post New Deal period altogether nevertheless avoided acknowledging that anything had really changed: 'Critics say that America is a lie because its reality falls far short of its ideals. They are wrong. America is not a lie; it is a disappointment. But it can be a disappointment only because it is also a hope' (Huntington 1982: 262).

One would have expected that the tortured logic of such statements would have been taken as clear evidence of an imminenet ideological crisis. In the event, no such crisis occurred. Instead, what I will call 'official America' responded to the trauma of discovering that capitalism could not be made to deliver opportunity for all by experiencing a prolonged fit of forgetfulness or social amnesia. This fit continues today and takes the form of an involuntary repetition of the claim that the United States is *the* land of opportunity, combined with an equally involuntary forgetting of the promise that had been made by all administrations since the New Deal, namely that government would actively strive to make opportunity available to the whole population. In other words, after the mid-1970s official America gave up on even trying to be in fact, as well as in name, what it had defined as 'modern'. It also therefore gave up on trying to make what it continued to insist was one of its most 'sacred' words – opportunity – refer to anything that might presage a significant improvement in the lives of millions of poor Americans. However, this very sacredness means that no mainstream politician can call the perfection of American society into question and hope to be elected. As with the absolutist state during the baroque period, awe is the proper attitude, just as 'shock and awe' has become the prefered mode of exercising power. The result is that, politically at least, the United States has entered the condition that Baudrillard (1995) has specified as 'hyperreality'. This is a condition in which the dominant visuality is one in which images are understood to produce objects in the minds of people with the result that, as with Disneyland, simulations are particularly valued as safer than, and even an improvement on, reality. Thus, 'choice' has replaced 'opportunity' at the core of official discourse. 'Choice' may seem like it is a synonym for 'opportunity' but in fact it is a simulation. This is because, whereas 'opportunity' refers to jobs and making money, 'choice' refers instead to consumption and spending money as if the latter were not dependent on the former. 'Choice' is consequently socially safer in that it does not carry any implication that anything needs to be broadened or equalized or therefore that anything need change as regards the disposition of power and resources. Finally, 'choice' is better than 'opportunity' since it is impossible to improve on freedom. Morever, once political discourse becomes a matter of producing and maintaining a simulation rather than promising and proving the attainment of measurable goals, it becomes part of the aesthetic realm and therefore it is both inappropriate and impossible to check its veracity. The result is that, again as with the baroque politics is personalized and therefore only aesthetic or emotional responses are encouraged in that citizens are only expected to say whether or not they like, or what they feel about, a particular statement and/or the person making it.

Individual political and social withdrawal as well as governmental retrenchment occured in Europe too but to a lesser degree and from much higher baselines of popular political involvement and social spending and therefore without the amnesiac after effect – even the Blair/Giddens 'third way' was constrained to at least present itself as a variety of social democracy and therefore as still committed to the active pursuit of social justice. Accordingly, the exchange of 'choice' for 'opportunity' still seems to be a difficult idea to sell in Europe: it remains strongly associated with ability to pay. (Who would freely choose an inferior house, school, or hospital?) Freedom is not the ethical absolute that it is in the United States since both the Christian and Social Democratic discourses of rule allow constraint in the communal interest. Consequently, and despite a determined and largely successful effort on the part of European politicians of all stripes to turn a blind eye to the pathologies intrinsic to capitalism, political discourse has not escaped into the realm of the aesthetic and remains therefore in the realm of the profane and the disputable – charges of hypocrisy and lying concerning a politician's governmental achievements remain far more potent political weapons than any allegations of personal impropriety.

Irrespective of the particular conditions they faced, it was initially very difficult for sociologists on either side of the Atlantic to know how to respond to these developments, because neither the classical paradigm nor its modernist offspring possessed, to use Foucault's vocabulary, the enunciative, conceptual or strategic resources to enable them to grasp what was going on. In such circumstances practitioners in any discipline commonly turn to neighbouring fields of enquiry for inspiration and even concepts. In this case, and especially in the American context, thanks to its understandable prominence in so individualistic a culture, the most obvious source of inspiration for puzzled sociologists, as well as disappointed individuals and groups, was psychology and the concept that was borrowed was that of identity.

Beginning in the 1930s, Freudian theory and its derivatives had turned individual identity, as a topic if not as a word, into a popular preoccupation, as instanced by the many films, novels and self-help books concerned with this theme. By the late 1970s, American sociologists, notably Richard Sennett (1977) and Christopher Lasch (1978), had produced historical and sociological explanations for the inward turn amongst their fellow citizens, which turn they both characterized in Freudian terms as 'narcissistic'. Deprived of their fathers by the demands of corporate America that had turned them into a 'lonely crowd' (Riesman 1950) of 'white collar' (Mills 1951) 'organization men' (Whyte 1963), and left alone with their housebound mothers (Friedan 1963), the postwar 'babyboomers' had grown up without having fully resolved their 'Oedipus complexes' and as a result had remained uncomfortably dependent on others for their sense of self. Such dark thoughts did not, however, appeal to the majority of either the disappointed or those who sought to understand them. Significantly, the conception of the person in terms of which this majority had come to think about such issues had also changed during the postwar period. Specifically, this conception had become much less associated with the resistant, almost biological thing represented by the Freudian unconscious and had instead become associated with a set of responsive and flexible cognitive faculties that could be used actively and positively to shape an identity and so make the ultimate personal choice.

Parsons' theory played a direct and highly significant role in this 'cognitive turn'. One of Parsons' psychologist colleagues at Harvard, Edward Tolman, was asked to contribute to the seminal book, *Toward a General*

Theory of Action (Parsons and Shils 1951) and as a result went on to become one of the founders of cognitive psychology. Reflecting on all the learning and adjustments individuals have to undertake in preparing themselves for, as well as performing, their roles, Tolman argued that one of the most important consequences for psychology of Parsonian theory was the new emphasis that it gave to 'thinking' which, significantly, he understood as a form of reflexivity:

> The process of thinking ... seems to consist in some type of internal activity which enables an actor to bring into play the consequences of given potential types of behavior without, however, actually carrying out these behaviors. And as a result of these brought-into-play consequences he modifies or reformulates or expands his behavior space and his belief-value matrix ... Satisfactory psychological studies of this *process* are as yet ... to be written.
>
> (Tolman 1951: 357, emphasis in original)

For the disappointed, their sociological sympathizers, and those anyway always ready to 'move on', the optimistic and modernistic cognitive psychologies that generalized Tolman's point about the importance of thinking were much more appealing than the old behaviouralist and Freudian psychologies (for the effect of the rise of cognitive psychology on the psychoanalytic tradition in the United States, see Rustin 2004). In the case of the disappointed as well as the reconciled, this was because the new psychologies provided intellectual and even scientific backing for the personalizing of their aspirations. In the case of the sociologists, it was also because the ground had been prepared by a burgeoning of interest during the 1960s in a long-established but hitherto marginal, cognate school of thought, symbolic interactionism, which was not only preoccupied with the production of the self, but had already spawned much work on subcultural identities.

The consequences of the changed nature of the sociological unthought that resulted from the cognitive nature of the inward turn were initially made visible in social theory by the attention paid to the concepts of 'action' and 'agency' over those of 'system' and 'structure'. The net result of this shift in interest has been the move towards solipsism that I regretted in my introduction. This move is most clearly and pertinently exemplified by the transformation in the conception of social structure that occurred within two still very influential bodies of theory that regard themselves as the concept's last best hope in what Charles Lemert (2004), bizarrely, has called the 'time after the structures disappeared'. The first of these is Anthony Giddens' 'structuration theory', wherein the dualism of subject and object or agent and structure is replaced by the what is claimed to be the 'duality of structure'. In a way that is both distinctly at odds with much of his earlier and indeed later work and largely unexplained, Giddens begins the book in which structuration theory is set out, *The Constitution of Society* (1984), by embracing the key propositions of what Lemert has called the 'new sociologies':

1   an emphasis on the 'active, reflexive character of human conduct';
2   the according of a 'fundamental role to language and to cognitive faculties in the explanation of social life';
3   'the declining importance of empiricist philosophies of natural science ... [which means] that a philosophy of natural science must take account of just those social phenomena in which the new schools of social theory are interested – in particular language and the interpretation of meaning'

[all passages are from Giddens, 1984: xvi]

On this basis he explains what he means by the 'duality of structure' in the following terms:

Human social activities, like some self-reproducing items in nature, are recursive. That is to say, they are not brought into being by social actors but continually recreated by them via the very means whereby they express themselves *as* actors. In and through their activities agents reproduce the conditions that make these activities possible.

(Giddens 1984: 2)

Because of its uncompromising humanism (in this context again the assumption that, in the end, all social stuff is reducible to individual human beings and their interactions) and the retreat from visuality to vision that it carries (Woodiwiss 2001: Chapter 2), such an ontology rules out in advance, because of their invisibility, the possibility that there may be forms of social life other than, or other to, human actors or entities reducible to them. Instead all there is to social life is 'agents ... [moving] in physical contexts whose properties interact with their capabilities ... at the same time as those agents interact with one another' (Woodiwiss 2001: 112). This becomes the core of Giddens' concept of structure except that, in a way reminiscent of Parsons' inclusion of 'means and conditions' within the 'unit act' and anticipating Latour's concept of 'quasi-objects' (see above, p. 69), he specifies 'rules and resources' as the 'physical contexts' of agents. But this is also the way in which social structure disappears from Giddens' theory and solipsism takes over – that is, social structure is reduced to rules and resources made or assembled by other or preceding actors in time-space and it is therefore 'out of time and space, save in its instantiations and coordination as memory traces' (Woodiwiss 2001: 25). If 'memory traces' in the minds of individuals are all that remain of social structure, what is the other to individual human beings that would justify any idea of the 'duality of structure'? Thus, since all of social life is in one's mind, and as Giddens seems to have decided practically if not formally, there is no need to look beyond one's own mind when trying to understand the social.

The second body of theory of particular interest as regards the fate of 'social structure' is 'neo-institutionalism', which continues to be one of the most influential 'formal theories' amongst American sociologists. The key thesis of the neo-institutionalists is what its adherents characterize as the mirror image of the 'actor-centrism' of the rational choice theory (for a parallel analysis to the present one focused on the rise of the concept of 'rational choice', see Amadae 2004) that appears to have captivated large numbers of economic and political theorists. This is the idea that society should be understood by sociologists as consisting not of actors but of 'organizations' or institutionalized 'knowledge and culture'. Thus the causal connections neo-institutionalism is interested in operate at the 'collective level and are cultural in nature – they feature processes occurring within and between institutions ... the people implicated are ... occupants of highly institutionally constructed roles, operating more in their cultural and professional capacities – that is, as *agents of the cultural system* – than as generic individual "actors"' (Jepperson 2002: 233, emphasis added). Neo-institutionalism, however, is explicitly rooted in phenomenology and consequently as it has developed, its conception of 'organizations' has tended to reduce to 'knowledge and culture' and agents have tended to reduce to actors. This is hardly surprising since neo-institutionalism's substantive research foci and understandings are every bit as Ameri-centric as those of Parsonianism. More specifically, neo-institutionalism bases itself on the following sustantive axioms: first, the United States is the archetypal modern society; and second, Western history is to be understood as a process of modernization or convergence on the American archetype thanks to the diffusion of American-style economic and political organizational forms – that is, 'the secularization and elaboration of individualism ... [is] ... the main theme in Western history' (Meyer 1986: 200). Thus, today's leading neo-institutionalists seem to have forgotten their opposition to 'actor centrism', lost interest in institutions *per se* and become preoccupied with the 'contemporary identity explosion' (Frank and Meyer 2000, quoted in Jepperson 2002: 250).

Conclusion

In sum, the unthought dimension of the picturing machine that is Atlanticist social theory was significantly shaped by ideas derived from the

United States' hegemonic, individualist ideology as mediated through the complex optical mechanism represented by the combination of the deployment of the concept of modernity, the privileging of the cultural sphere, the rise of cognitive psychology, the increased interest in 'action' and agency, the creation of identity theory, a shift from an empiricist/realist to a rationalist ontology, the practice of a subjectivist form of reflexivity, and the onset of a peculiarly American postmodernity.

8 The politicization of identity and the eclipse of class

The major immediate political danger to historiography today is 'antiuniversalism' or 'my truth is as valid as yours, whatever the evidence'. This appeals to various forms of identity group history, for which the central issue of history is not what happened but how it concerns the members of a particular group. What is important to this kind of history is not rational explanation but 'meaning', not what happened but what members of a collective group defining itself against outsiders – religious, ethnic, national, by gender or lifestyle – feel about it.

(Hobsbawm 'In defence of history')

Despite the fact that the psychologically-oriented resources represented by the identity theory that fertilized the 'new sociologies' and their distinctive stress on reflexivity were so close at hand, their take-up is not explainable by reference to purely intellectual developments alone, not least because many sociologists on both sides of the Atlantic, and not simply adherents to the classical tradition, strongly resisted any such take-up. Overcoming this resistance required both that existing concepts and strategies should be discredited and that authorities prepared to carry out such a task and push the new conceptual agenda should have emerged. As commonly happens in such circumstances, new intellectual spaces were created that were relatively free from the constraints of the established discursive formation. In this case, the principal spaces were feminism, and the overlapping, quasi-social movements called postmodernism and cultural studies. Great interest and excitement were aroused by the appearance of these new spaces, not least on the part of a publishing industry ever hungry for new product. The largely unintended result, as was illustrated in the previous chapter, was that many established social theorists quite suddenly, and with little by way of explanation, took up the new issues and concepts, forgot about the old ones, and thereby joined the politicians in their state of amnesia. In this case, however, what were forgotten were not only the promises of politicians but also the problems that the politicians had promised to solve.

Feminist epistemology: the political becomes personal

Perhaps the single most effective and memorable slogan associated with the feminist movement of the 1970s was 'the personal is political.' Incomplete though the feminist project remains, its achievements, especially in the societies of the global north, are nevertheless very substantial, not least within the spheres of sociology and social theory more generally, wherein women and their concerns have long since ceased to be marginal. That is, to use Jurgen Habermas' famous distinction, the so-called 'private sphere' of 'families' and intimate relations more generally is now regarded as every bit as important a focus of sociological interest as the 'public sphere' of, say, economic and political life. Likewise, the sources of gender inequality in the public sphere and the forces that maintain this inequality are another major focus of sociological interest. This said, it should also be acknowledged that, for a time at least, the rise of the 'women question' to social and sociological prominence contributed significantly to the subversion of the Durkheimian sociological project. This was because, to a far greater degree than the focus on racial and ethnic identities, the focus on women's collective identity stimulated a series of apparently radical challengers to the established or 'malestream' metatheoretical positions which, in so far as they were associated with an often very effective social movement, greatly strengthened and enhanced the plausibility of the inward turn.

Using Sandra Harding's (1986) typology, these challengers were feminist empiricism, feminist standpoint epistemology, and feminist postmodernism. For those categorized as feminist empiricists, science's neglect of women and their concerns was not in any way intrinsic to the empiricist understanding of the nature of scientific work. Rather, it simply reflected the fact that most scientists had been and remained men. Thus the key to correcting the neglect of women and their concerns was simply to ensure that more women became natural and social scientists. For the standpoint theorists and Harding herself, the feminist empiricist position was incoherent because it insisted both that the empiricist tradition was correct in the claims that it made for scientific objectivity and that this objectivity would be still enhanced further if the gender of the people doing the science was changed – if what the empiricist tradition terms the 'scientific method' necessarily produces objective results, why should changing the gender of those applying the method make any difference?

For Harding and the many other feminist scholars whose work she synthesized, their empiricist sisters were wrong about the objectivity of scientific method and right about gender making a difference to what was seen as a consequence of scientific work. Indeed the defining argument of the feminist standpoint epistemologists was that a female-guided and practised science would be a superior science to its male-dominated counterpart, especially in the social sciences. This was for at least three reasons. First, women have wider social experience than men (that is, they know about the private as well as the public sphere). Second, thanks to their wider experience, women have access to, and expertise in, a wider range of research strategies than men – more specifically, because of their experience of the private sphere women are likely to be especially skilful when deploying methods that require observers to empathize with those whom they are studying. Third, because of their experience of inequality, they are likely to be far more able than men to understand the experience and view of the world of other subordinated groups.

These arguments were soon challenged within feminist circles by those who disputed either the idea that there was one unitary feminist standpoint that transcended any differences of race, ethnicity, class, or culture, or the idea that there was anything very distinctive, let alone superior, about feminist science (Halberg, 1989). In the 1980s, the first type of critique was particularly influential thanks to the affinity between it and especially the social constructionist and therefore also the deconstructive aspects of postmodernism (see below and Tong, 1998). For the postmodernist feminists almost any claim to a specific gender identity represented simply the latest form of the anachronistic essentialism that the standpoint epistemologists in particular had criticized Marxism for with respect to class. In this way a movement that had begun by declaring that it would make the personal political for a time contributed significantly to a broader intellectual movement that made everything seem personal. By the 1990s, the second type of critique had come to the fore since the sheer productivity of feminist and female scholars more generally committed to any and none of these positions, as well as of those whom they influenced, including many male sociologists, meant that it became possible to talk about the existence of a sociology of gender. Having changed the substantive ontology of sociology and indeed cultural studies, it seems that the desire of female social scientists to proclaim epistemological difference has faded.

Postmodernism: everything becomes personal

Backtracking a little, postmodernism, like modernism, first emerged as an only partly intellectually self-conscious aesthetic stance. Beginning in the early 1960s, postmodernism challenged the orthodoxies of modernism in the arts. Its adherents rejected the modernist commitment to seeking after and attempting to represent the true or deeper nature of things by developing new and distinctive modes of representation in favour of working, for example, on

pre-existing or found images and mixing styles (*vide* the contrast between sur-
realism and pop art, www.artcyclopedia.com – search in 'Movements'). It
gradually became a more intellectually self-conscious movement as it entered
the academy (especially departments of architecture, art history, and literature) and became linked with a particular and most often idealist reading of
such post-structuralist writers as Roland Barthes, Jacques Lacan, Jacques
Derrida, and Foucault. These writers were regarded as radicalizing the significance of Saussure's rejection of the representationalist paradigm in linguistics
that Wittgenstein's first theory of language also exemplified (see above, pp.
99–101). Each was read as stressing, in his distinctive way, the positive analytical benefits of the actual or possible uncertainty of meaning consequent
upon the mutual irreducibility of signifiers, signifieds, and referents. If painting could no longer be judged on the basis of its contribution to the pursuit
of the ultimate truth about the world, nor could any other instance of communication, including political communication.

With the publication of Lyotard's *The Postmodern Condition* in 1979, the
movement became a fully self-conscious, pan-disciplinary 'anti-founda-
tionalism' that claimed to have transcended metaphysics as such (that is,
all ontologies and epistemologies). Thus the postmodernists saw themselves as a sign of times defined by a generalized 'incredulity towards [the]
metanarratives' that had hitherto underpinned the quest for knowledge.
What Lyotard means by this is that, whatever their differences, all modernist thinkers had shared a belief in two *grands recits*'(metanarratives) that
he terms the Myth of Truth and the Myth of Progress. The first of these
refers to the belief that the true nature of the world is knowable, whilst the
second refers to the belief that the pursuit of knowledge is good in itself
and should ultimately lead to a better world. For Lyotard, these are myths
in a strong cognitive sense in that both are demonstrably false. For him, the
belief that the true nature of the world is ultimately knowable was no
longer accepted by those who were supposed to know about these things,
namely the philosophers of science – he instances Kuhn (1970) in particular. Also, the belief in the inherently progressive nature of the pursuit of
knowledge had long ago been falsified by the role of the social and natural
sciences in the great crimes of the twentieth century: the Holocaust, the
Gulags, and the creation of weapons of indiscriminate mass destruction.
Moreover, according to Lyotard he was not the only one who knew the
modernist metanarratives to be false because it was the spontaneous spread
of such scepticism from the 1960s onwards that enabled him to describe
the times as postmodern. In the light of this transformation, he averred
that it would be best if we accepted with the later Wittgenstein that our sciences were simply a variety of 'language game' with no superior status to
any others and therefore to be judged solely according to their performa-
tivity or utility in solving practical problems. In other words, we should be
brave and try to find a way of not only thinking for ourselves but also, as

others have put it, reasoning without foundations or illusions.

Following Frederic Jameson (1991: Chapter 1), the differences between modernism and postmodernism may be summarized in the following terms:

> whereas modern artefacts – whether they are paintings, buildings or social theories – reflect a concern to uncover deep truths about the world, postmodern artefacts reflect, almost literally, a fascination with surfaces.

> whereas modern artefacts are the product of a desire to find the one true method or a pure style, postmodern artefacts seek to communicate through decoration and eclecticism;

> whereas modern artefacts attend to or reflect the forces that give structure or unity to the world, postmodern artefacts are much more reflective of fragmentation and difference;

> whereas modern artefacts tend to carry or are intended to stimulate, a strong emotional commitment, postmodern artefacts exemplify or commend a cooler, more detached and even ironic stance;

> whereas modern artefacts often point towards some future utopia, postmodern artefacts are intended to be immediately pleasurable.

As applied to social theory, and of course to oversimplify, modernist social theories focus on uncovering deep truths, proselytize on behalf of one or other version of the one true method, find their truths in such unitary forms as those represented by social structure, class, bureaucracy and the division of labour, require or seek a high level of emotional commitment, and point towards a better future. By contrast, postmodernist social theories are preoccupied with the appearance of things (hence their focus on the media and culture more generally), reject any claims for the superiority of any particular method, exhibit great interest in bodily differences such as those associated with race, sexual orientation, gender and the identities they consider to be related to these differences, advise that nothing should be taken too seriously because disappointment is more likely than satisfaction, and recommend that no opportunity for pleasure should be passed up.

If, for the sake of argument, the accuracy of this representation of the theoretical alternatives is granted, and even considering postmodernism from a modernist perspective, there seems little to object to in the individual distinctive features and interests of postmodernism. The problem, or so it seems to me, is that, when taken together, read as requiring an entirely new visualization of contemporary social life, and confused with an equally care-lessly understood social constructionism, as they were by the popularizers and their dependents, they were taken as evidence that the things that the modernists were interested in no longer existed. Moreover, ironically and dis-appointingly, even the postmodernist masters such as Foucault, Baudrillard and Lyotard, who all in fact refused the label, failed to extend the scope of their 'incredulity' to include the pondering of either the reasons for their own sudden prominence or the neglect of those ideas of theirs, such as 'dis-cursive formations' and 'hyperreality', that could have explained the largely uncommented upon nature of the transformation of American official dis-course. Also, it soon became apparent within cultural studies that a bowdler-ized postmodernism was the required position if someone wished to be regarded as taking the cultural sphere plus issues of 'race', gender and sexu-ality seriously. In this way, many problems that had formerly been under-stood by sociologists and others as matters of economic inequality came to be understood instead as matters of culture or insufficiently developed or assertive identities, and, increasingly, as requiring psychological intervention rather than the support of a welfare state.

Idealizing discourse

As I implied at the end of my outline of Foucault's contribution to the development of a realist reflexivity, a funny thing happened to the concept of discourse on its way to the theory and methodology textbooks. I have argued elsewhere that many secondary theory texts wrongly present the concept of discourse as the product or instrument of an idealism (Woodiwiss 2001: Chapter 4) so I will not repeat this argument here. Instead I will simply reinforce the point by briefly looking at how discourse theory was and is presented in some leading methodology textbooks. In Potter and Wetherell (1987), which for a long time was the only book one could turn to if one wanted to know how to do discourse analysis, the fol-lowing may be found:

> Participants' discourse or social texts are approached in their own right and not as a secondary route to things 'beyond' the text like attitudes, events or cognitive processes. Discourse is treated as a potent, action-orientated medium, not a transparent information channel. Crucial questions for traditional social psychological research thus cease to be relevant. For example, we are not asking whether a sample of people are revealing their 'genuine' attitudes to ethnic minorities, or whether fans' descriptions of what happens on the soccer terraces are 'accurate'. The concern is exclu-

sively with talk and writing itself and how it can be read, not with descriptive acuity ...

Interviews, however, are a very different tool for discourse analysts than for orthodox social researchers. The goal of traditional interviews is to obtain or measure consistency in participants' responses; consistency is valued so highly because it is taken as evidence of a corresponding set of actions or beliefs. If the interview talk is consistent, the argument goes, it must reflect a consistent reality beyond; consistent discourse demonstrates the interviewer has found some genuine phenomena and not biased or distorted responses.

(Potter and Wetherell 1987: 160–3, references removed)

In short, the clear message is that the concept of discourse is part of a rationalist idealist theoretical package.

The same thing is true of Fran Tonkiss's otherwise excellent contribution to Clive Seale's *Researching Society and Culture* (1998):

While 'discourse' may be used loosely to refer to any text or utterance, in this discussion I will be employing it in a more formal way. In this context, 'discourse' refers to *a system of language* which draws on a particular terminology and encodes specific forms of knowledge. The easiest way to understand this idea is to think about the example of 'expert' languages. Doctors, for example, do not simply draw on their practical training when doing their job; they also draw on an expert medical language that allows them to identify symptoms, make diagnoses and prescribe remedies. This language is not readily available to people who are not medically trained. Such an expert language has three important effects: *it marks out a field of knowledge; it confers membership; and it bestows authority ... Secondly, ... discourse allows [experts] to communicate with each other in coherent and consistent ways ... Thirdly, ... discourse authorizes certain speakers and statements ...* [In such cases] the analyst is concerned not so much with getting at the truth of an underlying social reality through discourse, but with examining the way that language is used to present different 'pictures' of reality.

(Tonkiss 1998: 248–9, emphasis added)

The problem here is that the effects listed in the italicized part of the extract are understood by Foucault to be the product of a discursive formation which, as was made clear above (see pp. 101–3), involves much more than a discourse in the sense of a 'system of language'.

And just in case there is any doubt about the degree of continuing methodological consensus on the matter, here is Alan Bryman's very recent and only slightly hesitant confirmation in his characterization of discourse analysis:

- It is anti-realist, in other words, it denies that there is an external reality awaiting a definitive portrayal by the researcher and it therefore disavows the notion that any researcher can arrive at a privileged account of the aspect of the social world being investigated. Some discourse analysts, however, adopt a stance that is closer to a realist position, but most seem to be anti-realist in orientation.

- It is constructionist, in other words, the emphasis is placed on the versions of reality propounded by members of the social setting being investigated and on *the fashioning of that reality through their renditions of it*. More specifically, the constructionist emphasis entails a recognition that discourse entails a selection from many viable renditions and that in the process a particular depiction of reality is built up.

(Bryman 2004: 360)

In sum, then, thanks to the postmodernist popularizers and others the category of discourse was cut adrift from that of discursive formation with the result that, instead of providing a way to understand the socially rooted nature of knowledge that nevertheless acknowledges the possibility of purely discursive effects, it came to be understood as referring to the way in which social actors escape their social circumstances, project their desires onto social life and thereby create it.

Losing sight of class

Britons in general and British sociologists in particular were, and possibly still are, thought, by Americans especially, to be obsessed with class as the core component of the social structure. In my view, both groups of Britons were and still should be so obsessed and for good sociological as well as social reasons. This said, stimulated by the phenomena that came to be called Thatcherism, a debate, which in part was transatlantic, raged during the 1980s concerning whether or not the salience of class was decreasing in contemporary British society. In what follows, and from the vantage point provided by the account of changes to the pertinent discursive formation provided above, I will outline this debate with a view to specifying exactly how class was eclipsed by identity within the pictures of social life produced by social theorists.

Among the sets of ideas that structured the British debate were the various suggestions to the effect that the 1980s were what Bell (1976) called 'interstitial times' or what the Communist Party of Great Britain, more simply, called 'New Times'. One conclusion frequently drawn by such prophets was that this ongoing transitional process rather sharply called into question the continuing salience of class theory as a means of understanding advanced capitalist societies (not a novel thesis as regards the United States, of course). For the advocates of what became known as the post-industrial society thesis, like Bell, the ever-increasing economic importance of what might be called 'intellectual means of production' promised to shrink radically, if not completely dissolve, the working class by greatly increasing the size of the so-called 'middle class'. For the advocates of the postmodernity thesis, and to a certain extent for advocates of the post-industrial society thesis such as Bell too, the 1970s had been characterized by a belated realization that the world of facts and the world of discourse had already become autonomous of one another. According to such thinkers, this meant that some people had already begun to construct social identities for themselves in place of those hitherto foisted upon them by the class structure; and all this despite the non-occurrence of the revolution that for the Marxist tradition was supposed to be the prerequisite for the replacement of the realm of necessity by that of freedom.

Perhaps the best-known application of the post-industrial society thesis to the question of class in Britain is Ivor Crewe's 'dealignment thesis'. According to Crewe (1986), class has become an ever less dependable predictor of how people will vote, as social mobility, home ownership, private consumption and, therefore, the size of the middle class have each increased. And it was because of this that, between 1945 and 1983, the Conservative Party's share of the middle-class vote in general elections fell from 63 per cent to 55 per cent, whilst the Labour Party's share of the working class vote fell even more steeply from 62 per cent to 42 per cent. Perhaps the best known application of the postmodernity thesis to questions of class in Britain is contained in Stuart Hall's (1985; 1988) analysis of the discourse of Thatcherism, which combines some postmodernist ideas with others derived from the more economically orientated neo-Marxist theories of 'postfordism' (see Aglietta 1976 and Lipietz 1985, for example). According to Hall, one important reason why the Conservatives were electorally much more successful than Labour in the 1980s was because Thatcherism, like the market-led, postfordist capitalist enterprises it served, was a discourse based upon an acknowledgement of the contemporary fluidity of social identities that had yet to be made by the Labour Party. Thus, argues Hall, the Conservatives under Thatcher designed their policies in such a way that they appealed not only to their traditional supporters, but also to skilled manual workers in fordist and postfordist factories, as well as to other formerly loyal Labour supporters who preferred to think themselves as individuals rather than as members of a class. Each of the latter groups is, therefore, understood to have been grateful to the Conservatives for policies such as council house sales, privatization and the associated broadening of share-ownership, increased educational choice, anti-permissiveness, and a more aggressive foreign policy. And each of these policies had, in turn, supposedly helped the beneficiaries of these policies to feel like the independent, financially and socially secure, as well as patriotic, citizens they wished to be. In the meantime, Hall argues, not only had Labour failed to counter this appeal but it had also failed to respond positively enough to the new demands raised by the emerging new constituencies of people who identified themselves not in class terms but by reference to their 'race', their femaleness, and/or their sexual orientation. Indeed, not only had Labour failed to capture the support of these constituencies by not responding positively enough to them, but also, because it had in fact offered some lukewarm support to some of the demands raised by some of them, it had further alienated the discursively Thatcherized section of the traditional working class.

In sum, the challenges to traditional class analysis, whether in its Marxist or Weberian forms, were twofold: first, the class structure was changing shape, essentially from a pyramidal to a diamond form, and at an accelerating pace; and second, the class structure as a largely economic construct had been displaced from its position of structural primacy by political and ideological/cultural discourses, namely identities, which had gained a social salience that was increasingly independent of any connections that such constructs may or may not once have had with economic or class constructs.

This, then, was how class was challenged by the rise of identity theory. However, if one wishes to understand fully how the latter eclipsed the former, the response by the partisans of class has also to be examined. Amongst the more orthodox Marxists, the main line of defence was to cast doubt upon the empirical grounds for these challenges and on this basis to resist the idea that there was any need for theoretical innovation. Underlying this stance was a continuing commitment to the idea of the long-run proletarianization of the labour force, most often associated with the name of Harry Braverman (1974). In the United States, perhaps the best-known writer associated with this position was Mike Davis (1986), while in Britain it was Alex Callinicos (Callinicos and Harman 1987; Callinicos 1989). For Callinicos, drawing on Davis, the post-industrialism thesis as it affected the class structure is largely a mirage. Service-sector employment had increased in Britain and the United States, but this had not meant that white-collar or 'middle-class' employment had increased to the same degree because the service sector included many manual workers (in the fast food industry, for example). Moreover, even if the manufacturing labour force had shrunk this was only as a proportion of the total labour force and not as an absolute number. And, finally, if many workers no longer voted for the Democratic or Labour Parties, this was because those parties had long since given up even pretending to represent the interests of ordinary wage earners. Similarly, Davis and Callinicos have little time for the idea of postfordism let alone that of postmodernism. Callinicos, in particular, finds the contrast between fordism and postfordism to be greatly exaggerated. This is because, as he sees it, mass production had always been heavily dependent on the market-creating effects of advertising, often involving short production runs, and any way continued to be a very important employment sector. Moreover, neither British nor indeed American industry exhibited many signs of either the arrival of 'flexible specialization', or of any special privileging of the so-called 'core' workforce. Additionally, Davis and Callinicos regard the significance of the rise of the new, identity-based social movements, although not the significance of their demands, as being greatly exaggerated and, more than anything else, to be a reflection of a certain compensatory wishful thinking on the part of the disappointed radicals of the 1960s.

Neo-Weberians were, then, a far more conspicuous feature of the British sociological landscape than of the American. This said, despite many conceptual differences but unsurprisingly given his adoption of some of the 'rational choice' ideas of John Roemer, Erik Olin Wright (1985) adopts a position which implies a very similar defence of the continuing salience of class analysis for understanding the American social formation to that which the neo-Weberians had suggested as regards Britain. This is a defence that is similar to that of the orthodox Marxists, except that it involves not so much a denial of the new facts espied by the theorists of post-industrial society and postmodernity as a questioning of their novelty and of some of the conclusions drawn from them. The defence of class analysis mounted by Gordon Marshall et al. (1989) is explicit, whereas that present in Wright's work remains largely implicit, and so Marshall et al.'s defence is the one that I will now outline. For Marshall et al., neither the allegedly changing shape of the British class structure, the discovery of individualism among the working class, the new salience of non-class social identities such as those associated with gender, nor, finally, Labour's loss of the previous three elections pose any serious problems for their mode of analysis; indeed they find their approach to have been thoroughly vindicated by these developments.

In agreement with one of their mentors, John Goldthorpe (1980), Marshall et al. do not accept the post-industrial society thesis that there had been any great increase in social mobility in postwar Britain. In any event, they are not discomfited by arguments that stress the importance of 'middle-class' positions in the class structure. This is because Weberian class analysis had long stressed the importance of what David Lockwood (1958) was the first to term 'market situation' and 'work situation' as codeterminants of class position alongside property ownership/non-ownership. Thus the class 'map' they adopt, which is Goldthorpe's, is diamond shaped, even if the distribution of persons between its categories is not. Likewise, Marshall *et al.* are not at all discomfited by the attention paid to working-class individualism, the emergence of new social identities and the occurrence of Conservative voting among the working class. And again, this is because Weberian class analysis had always assumed that the cultural and political dimensions of class have an autonomy from its economic dimension. As regards these issues, they argue as follows: 1) working-class individualism, as exemplified by the nineteenth-century labour aristocracy of skilled workers, is as old as the working class, and it does not necessarily rule out the possibility of solidaristic beliefs and actions among its practitioners (*vide* the role of the labour aristocracy in the formation of unions of unskilled labourers in the latter part of the nineteenth century); 2) the significance of the new social identities as a solvent of class identities has been greatly exaggerated, because, for example, most women take their class identity from their husband's occupation rather than from their own; and, finally, 3) the decline of the Labour Party's share of the vote has been a consequence of the reduction in the size of the manual working class as a proportion of the labour force from 47 per cent to 34 per cent, and of political failures (different from those identified by Callinicos, of course) on the part of the Labour Party rather than of any disintegration of the class structure. In sum, both Marxists and Weberians felt that the events of the recent past had confirmed rather than undermined the utility of their basic theoretical approaches.

By contrast, in my view what I have just outlined is a story of missed opportunities. Regardless of what one thinks the answers should be, the questions posed by the events of the Thatcher and, indeed, Reagan years should have prompted a far more radical rethinking of class theory than is apparent in the texts I have just discussed. The critics of the orthodoxies of class analysis did not provide alternative conceptualizations that are at all developed, whilst the defenders of the orthodoxies responded exactly as Thomas Kuhn predicts people in such a position will always respond, namely by making *ad hoc* alterations to less central parts of their theories (in this instance their class 'maps') in order to protect the more central parts.

To develop the point, what it seems to me that the dispute between the critics and the guardians of the orthodoxies was fundamentally about was the degree to which individual beliefs and behaviours are constrained by the class structure. For all the participants in the debate, including the postmodernistically inclined, it is individuals or groups of them who take up positions in the social relations of production (according to the Marxists) or in the occupational structure (according to the neo-Weberians), and who supposedly then translate (with varying degrees of predictability) the effects of these positions and occupations into political and ideological/cultural class effects. The critics argued that such constraints and translation effects were lessening and they sometimes also doubted that they had ever been very great. Meanwhile, the guardians of the orthodoxies responded that such constraints and translation effects remained as powerful as they ever were, even if they had not been properly understood before.

In sum, then, after examining the arguments and evidence provided by both sides, my conclusion is not that one side was right and the other wrong, but rather that there was more agreement between them than either side imagined and that this agreement could not be acknowledged because both sides made the same basic mistake. What they agreed about was that the beliefs and behaviour of individuals are far less predictable than sociologists had hitherto assumed. The critics gave reasons for this that have already been outlined, while the defenders of the orthodoxies unconsciously acknow-ledged it by refining and elaborating their class 'maps' and so increasing the likelihood that any particular combination of economic, ideological/cultural and political positions that an individual might take up may corres-pond to one or other of a set of predefined class categories. It was not so long ago that sociologists worked with two, three or four classes and/or strata. Now, in a manner that to me should have evoked Ockham's Razor (the precept that simplicity should be preferred to complexity), they sometimes work with six (early Wright), 11 (Goldthorpe) or 12 (later Wright) such categories.

The adoption of the latter mode of defence, the fact that, despite the proliferation of categories, it remained and indeed remains very difficult to make unambiguous assignments of some individuals and/or occupations to classes and/or strata, and the analytically crippling consequences of Marshall et al.'s (1989: 190–1) admirably frank admission of the impermissibility of drawing conclusions about individual beliefs on the basis of data concerning the distribution and structuring of beliefs within groups, all point in one direction, or so it seems to me. That is, they tend to confirm the point, which, sometimes knowingly, sometimes not, gave the critics' various positions their bite, namely that it is, and perhaps always has been, very difficult both to distinguish one person's class position from that of another, and to know anything about the relations between individual economic locations and individual beliefs. Thus the problems encountered as a result of trying to ground a theory of class on the classification of individuals or families defeated even the best efforts of some of the most methodologically and theoretically sophisticated sociologists of their generation.

The debate, of course, continued during the 1990s and continues still today. These later developments have recently been lucidly described and analysed by Wendy Bottero (2004). For this reason, I will say little about them here, except that the place, but certainly not the position, of the postmodernists in the debate has been taken by advocates of what has been termed 'culturalist class theory', notably Fiona Devine (1992; 1998; 2000) and Mike Savage (2000a; 2000b). Bottero has neatly summarized the core theses of what is a richly empirical argument of a neo-classical kind in the following terms:

> People do not have to explicitly recognize class issues, or identify with discrete class groupings, for class processes to operate. All that is required is for specific class practices to be bound up with the reproduction of hierarchy. The emphasis is not on the development (or not) of class consciousness, but rather on the classed nature of particular practices ... [consequently] individualization does not entail the death of class, but rather a shift in how class operates, for 'while collective class identities are indeed weak, people continue to define their own individual identities in ways that involve comparisons with members of other social classes' (Savage 2000: xii).
>
> (Bottero 2004: 989 references removed)

Should, though, the purpose of class analysis still be regarded as the vision-based one of classifying individuals and producing ever more complicated class 'maps'? I think not. It seems to me that, while particular practices may undoubtedly be 'classed' as Bourdieu (1984) has argued, individual people are always too unpredictable even in their 'comparisons with members of other social classes' to be ever usefully so categorized, and therefore for the categories so produced to provide any sort of firm basis for sociological reasoning. This unpredictability may only be elucidated by recourse to psychology (Woodiwiss 1990a: 25–7). The shared mistake, in my view, of all the participants in the debate I have outlined has been to think that either the individual or a collection of individuals should be the unit of class analysis, and has been to replicate in a certain sense Parson's search for the 'unit act' and look for a supposedly self-evidently visible 'unit of class analysis'. Instead of pursuing this approach, and in the light of the fact that theorizing is a matter of constructing visualities rather than one that is vision based, we should follow Durkheim's advice and rededicate ourselves to the task of uncovering, making visible and investigating otherwise invisible entities, forces and structures that are social in a *sui generis* sense. In the case of class, this means that we should be developing the concepts necessary to model the class structure as a specific set of interactions between economic, political and cultural relations. A set that socially produces and sociologically explains the particular salience of the structure of the ownership, control and administration of property in the means of production for the patterns of social inequality and therefore the life chances of those individuals who are affected by these patterns (Woodiwiss 1990a; 1992; 1993; 1998).

Conclusion

Just as the privileging and disprivileging of the classical texts in general and of the concept of class in particular were products of complex sets of changes within, and tensions between, the rules of formation of the discipline, as the latter continue to change and the tensions between them either relax, intensify or change their loci, so different discourses or schools within the discipline wax and wane in popularity and/or change in their foci. No one element in a discursive formation nor any one of its rules of formation is ultimately determinant of discursive outcomes. For example, sometimes the succession of concepts, and so forth, follows changes with respect to objects as in the case of classical theory. Sometimes it does not, as in the case of Parsonian sociology's inability to maintain the theoretical acknowledgement of the particularity of the capitalist economy. Sometimes changes in the conceptions of objects are prompted by changes with respect to enunciative modalities. Sometimes they are not, as is instanced by the recent disappearance of postmodernism long before it had had a chance to permanently change the way in which the world is understood.

Class, then, was eclipsed by identity within social theory over the course of the last two decades of the twentieth century as a result of the largely unwilled effects of the interaction between the different elements of sociology's unthought or discursive formation, as outlined in the preceding chapter (see Figure 8.1). First, as an object, sociology became the product of an Atlanticist institutional setting that was continuously transforming itself as the United States changed from being one of two superpowers to being the sole superpower as well as, in ideological terms, changing from being a modern society to being a postmodern society. Second, via the prior transformation of the basic picture of society from that of a structural ensemble

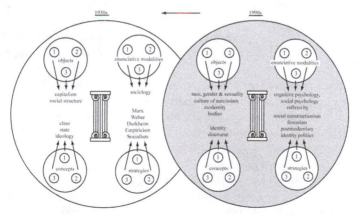

Figure 8.1 The rise of identity theory and the eclipse of class (viewed archaeologically)

to an 'action system', the central places of 'social structure' and 'class' within sociology's conceptual vocabulary were displaced by the concepts of culture, discourse, and identity. Third, as a style of talking and writing, soci- ology became ever more culturalist, psychologistic and reflexive. And fourth, strategically the intellectual running was made by an activist femi- nism and an idealist postmodernism, both of which sought the total re-the- orization of social life in a way that completely marginalized the study of capitalism and its pathologies.

Given all this, one of the more disturbing things about the rise of an Atlanticist social theory constructed around the concept of identity is the way in which many of its producers and readers still feel and indeed stress that it is critical or progressive in its political implications. Thus the testi- mony or reflections and speculations of those whom the highly influential social-constructionist Charles Lemert (2004: 208–11) has christened 'extra- sociological sociologists' – that is, various feminist, African-American and postcolonial writers *who tell the story of the world as it is* – are taken not simply as evidence for the reality and overwhelming social importance of identity but also as guarantees of the political progressiveness of the dis- course constructed around identity:

> For the lesbian of color, the ultimate rebellion she can make against her native culture is through her sexual behavior. She goes against two moral prohibitions: sexuality and homosexuality. Being lesbian and raised Catholic, indoctrinated as straight, I *made the choice to be queer* ... It's an interesting path, one that slips in and out of the white, the Catholic, the Mexican, the indigenous, the instincts. In and out of my head. It makes for *loqueria*, the crazies. It is a path of knowledge – one of knowing (and of learning) the history of oppression of our *raza*. It is a way of balancing, of miti- gating duality.
>
> (Gloria Anzaldua, quoted in Lemert 2004: 210,
> emphasis in the original)

Such testaments are, of course, to be respected as personal and political statements, and I would agree that many social activists as well as theorists took up the ideas associated with action, agency, identity theory and even postmodernism in the hope that these ideas would enhance their political effectiveness. However, and as she and Lemert's other recruits to the pro- fession may well themselves agree, to take such statements as Anzaldua's at face value and therefore as proof of the truth and progressive nature of identity discourse is, rather precisely, to turn sociology into a solipsistic and even therapeutic activity. Whether the argument is that society is what people feel it to be or is not what they feel it should be, the problem is the same. And it is that both arguments suggest that, in the same way that the

United States' 'social religions' (Berger, 1967) provide psychological support rather than theological enlightenment for their members, so sociology should provide people with the validation of themselves that no longer comes from participation in social life rather than provide them with explanations for society's failure to provide this validation. To me, what is nearly as dispiriting as the travails Anzaldua alludes to is the fact that her sociological sympathizer, at least in the 1995 edition of his book, appears neither to have inquired into why she should give so much positive emphasis to the statement that she *'made the choice to be queer'*, nor into why it is so easy to make such a statement in the United States but so difficult for many people to live the life it anticipates. The answer to both of these questions, or so it seems to me, is that, given the absence of any alternative to compare it with, and thanks now not so much to the fetishism of commodities as to a fetishism of consumption whose key sign is 'choice', capitalism as a *sui generis* set of interacting structures is currently almost invisible with the result that it is once again extremely difficult to see the source of its power – so difficult indeed that neo-conservative Republicans can win elections claiming to be representing the values and interests of the working class (Frank 2000, 2005). Thus, contra Lemert and the Atlanticist social theory he so winningly represented in 1995, it is not that the structures have disappeared but that they have once again been obscured from view by the lives they require people, including social scientists, to live, and pay for.

All this said, the rules of formation of the discursive formation never stop changing.

9 Globalization and the reappearance of social structure

Not only do the rules of formation of discursive formations keep changing, but they are also implacable in that, confirming the realist thesis that society is not simply a set of projected mentalistic phenomena but a living thing in its own right, no discourse can maintain its influence for long once the rules turn against it, so to speak. This appears to be particularly true of discourses that have gained a special degree of prominence, because such a position indicates that they suited their times (that is, the character and balance of social and intellectual forces) particularly well. This is a condition that, almost by definition, cannot last for long. Just as it is said of today's media in relation to celebrities, 'what they raise up they may also tear down', so it is with the rules of formation of discursive formations, except that the process of decline tends to be much more drawn out than in the case of celebrities. Thus, the same initial set of developments that brought the discourse of identity to the fore has since gone on to render that discourse passé as other consequences of these ongoing developments have brought new forces into play. In particular, the same set of problematic, America-centred developments with respect to the economy, social order and failed attempts at progressive social change that accounted for the onset of America's postmodernity and therefore made identity seem so salient a theoretical theme, was produced by and accelerated the process that was soon to become known as globalization:

> A period of prolonged economic growth and full employment in the advanced countries, sustained by active national state intervention and a managed multilateral regime for trade and monetary policy under US hegemony, was brought to an end [in the 1970s] by a number of significant changes [oil price rises, ending of fixed exchange rates, growth of international banking, deregulation of international financial markets, deindustrialization of the North and new industrialization in some parts of the South] ... [Consequently] the later 1980s and 1990s have been dominated by a consensus based on ...[the] assumptions that global markets are

uncontrollable and that the only way to avoid becoming a loser – whether as nation, firm or individual – is to be as competitive as possible.

(Hirst and Thompson 1999: 5–6)

The challenge represented by the sudden awareness that this complex of events brought about with respect to what had in fact (*pace* Hirst and Thompson) been a long-established process was one that, as even so committed a social constructionist as Lemert (2004: Chapter 10) now acknowledges, Atlanticist social theory was ill-equiped to throw any light on, precisely because of its intensifying preoccupation with intrasocietal individual/society relations rather than intersocietal relations. Thus not only have European scholars been much more interested in globalization than their American counterparts, but the Atlanticist theories that were so influential in the 1980s and 1990s, notably structuration theory, postmodernism and neo-institutionalism, have had little to say of lasting analytical significance about globalization. Those commited to the first two theories have tended to respond to globalization descriptively and have therefore tended to see it as the transnationalization of everything, whereas the third theory tends to reduce societal differences, like everything else, to matters of culture. By contrast, in my view, the analytically significant running has been made by scholars with strong roots in the more structurally oriented side of classical social theory like Immanuel Wallerstein (Marx), Michael Mann (Weber), Bob Jessop (Marx), Roland Robertson (Durkheim), Fred Halliday (Marx), and Ruccio *et al.* (Marx). To Wallerstein (2004), we owe the very idea of a global system. To Mann (1986), we owe the insight as to the inherently and inexhaustibly, if not exhaustive, transnational nature of social relations. To Jessop (1980), we owe an insight as to the sociological nature of the state and the consequent multiplicity of its interfaces with its national, international and transnational environments. To Halliday (1994), we owe the insight as to the extreme porosity of national boundaries that is apparent once Mann and Jessop's insights are combined. To Ruccio *et al.* (1991), we owe the insight that this porosity applies equally to the relations that are constitutive of the class structure and indeed, by extension, to all the other dimensions of social structures. And to Robertson (1990), we owe our most acute understanding of the specificity of globalization as a particular set of social relations and institutions.

This is not the place to justify the judgements just made nor to provide a general discussion of either globalization as a substantive process or attempts to theorize it (but see Woodiwiss 1998: Chapter 1; 2001: conclusion), because my concern here is to make some general points about the consequences of globalization for the inner structure and content of social theory. However, I would like to begin by acknowledging that, although the main argument in this chapter will be that the net effect of globalization on social theory is most likely to be the displacement of the problematic of identity by that of social structure, and even class, the more popular literature concerning globalization has thus far been strongly marked by issues of identity. Thus, prompted geopolitically by the collapse of communism and theoretically by Giddens (1990), who on this issue as well as many others does not seem to apply his own structuration theory, the debate initially revolved around whether or not globalization in general was a process of Westernization or even Americanization. More specifically, and as an example, the debate concerning cultural globalization (Tomlinson 1999) rapidly polarized around the issue of whether the result of globalization would be the destruction of national identities (the cultural imperialism thesis) or the multiplication of hybrid identities (the postcolonialist thesis).

At the time of writing, the apparent salience of identity issues has been given a new lease of life, if that is the appropriate term, by talk of a 'clash of civilisations' (Huntington 1997) and especially by the decision of the United States government and its allies to attack and occupy Iraq with its apparently unanticipated consequences in terms of the reanimation of non-Western nationalisms as assertions of dignity and autonomy. This said, and whether in the pursuit of knowledge or as a consequence of a forced withdrawal from Iraq, in the longer term the theoretical effects of such assertions seem likely to direct practitioners and therefore theoretical commentators towards issues concerning the resilience of the social-structural differences that give credence to the possibility of such nationalisms. Tragically, this shift was not well enough established to have represented much of an obstacle to sociologically naive ideas of 'regime change'. However, the shift has already occured in relation to certain Asian countries, notably Japan and the newly industrializing countries of Pacific Asia. Thus once again, developments on the margins of the discursive formation pertinent to social theory, and in this case also on the margins of the civilized world as far as most people in the West are concerned, seem likely to result in a transformation of the conceptual core of social theory (for what is in many ways a parallel analysis that focuses on Eastern Europe and Russia but arrives at similar conclusions to the present study, see William Outhwaite and Larry Ray's, *Social Theory and Postcommunism*, 2005). In the current instance this is because, contrary to those who argue that it involves the transnationalization of everything, globalization has made a range of social-structural arrangements that were at best peripheral to, but most often excluded from, the concerns of social theorists because of their supposedly barbaric character, suddenly central to the nature of the social-structural and institutional nexus within which the objects of interest to social theorists are defined and problematized:

Sociology as a discursive formation, as a system of power/knowledge was in part created by othering and/or denigrating 'Asia' as an object of study in order to bring the particularity of the 'West' into sharper focus.

Thus Marx defined the specificity of Western capitalist societies by contrasting them not only to their feudal predecessors but also to those of Asia, via the concept of the 'asiatic mode of production' or what Karl Wittfogel (1957) later termed 'oriental despotism'. Weber discovered the role of Protestantism in the rise of capitalism in the West not simply by contrasting it to Catholicism and Judaism but also by contrasting all three of them to Confucianism. Finally, less explicitly but unmistakeably nonetheless, Durkheim explained the relatively high level of the division of labour in the West by pointing to the more rapid weakening of the 'conscience collective' in the West than in the East.

By these different means, then, the West was defined as more economically (Marx), politically (Weber) and morally (Durkheim) advanced than the East and therefore, silently, more worthy of study.

(Woodiwiss 2001: 172)

It is hardly surprising, then, that, as Jeffrey Alexander has pointed out, 'Modernization' theory as such was born with the publication of Marion Levy's (1949) book on the Chinese family structure. Significantly, 1949 was also the year in which, according to Senator Joseph McCarthy and his supporters, the United States' State Department 'lost' China.

Returning to the present, the 'economic miracles' that alongside globalization account for the ending of the re-emphasis on Asia's exclusion from the 'modern' world that had followed the communist revolution in China also mean that Pacific Asia are often perceived in the West as somewhat threatening, and consequently knowledge of the particularities of such societies has gained a strategic significance for Western political and economic actors that it has not had since the nineteenth century and the era of competitive imperialisms. With such significant changes in what might be termed the input (globalization) and output (strategic utility) dimensions of its discursive formation, it is not surprising that conceptual change or at least reordering should be occuring within social theory.

At the same time as globalization has been making it increasingly important for sociologists to come to terms with the social differences represented by, for example, Pacific-Asian societies, theoretical work of a neo-classical kind has continued on the margins of the new, identity-centred orthodoxy. Significantly, or so it seems to me, this work has had its most fruitful outcome with respect to our understanding of social structure. Thus at the metatheoretical level, John Holmwood (1996) has explained how the hegemony of the agency/structure problematic in the 1970s and 1980s prevented the production of adequate structural models and explanations by allowing unexpected occurences to be explained away through the invocation of the contingent nature of agency, rather than using them to prompt further theoretical development. More recently, the same idea has been taken up by Jose Lopez (2003) and used to do two things. First, to criticize existing readings of the major theorists in the classical tradition, insofar as their readings are informed by the agency/structure problematic. And, second, to produce his own more purely structurally focused and highly suggestive readings of the classical theorists' now apparently forgotten thoughts as regards the nature of social structure. In another work, Lopez and his co-author John Scott usefully distinguish two senses in which the term 'structure' has been used in sociology:

> If structure is to be understood, for a moment, to mean pattern or arrangement – as opposed to that which is 'random' or 'chaotic' – then our aim is to see in exactly what ways the pattern or arrangement of social life has been understood.
>
> ... the history of sociology shows the long term coexistence of two different conceptions of social structure. On the one hand, there is that which we identify as the idea of *institutional* structure. Here, social structure is seen as comprising those cultural or normative patterns that define the expectations that agents hold about each other's behaviour and that organize their enduring relations with each other. On the other hand, there is the idea of what we call *relational* structure. Here, social structure is seen as comprising the social relations themselves, understood as patterns of causal interconnection and interdependence among agents and their actions, as well as the positions that they occupy.
>
> (Lopez and Scott 2000: 3)

Insightfully, they add:

> Debates in theoretical and empirical sociology have, in large part, been shaped by the rivalry between the advocates of these two different concepts of social structure.
>
> (Lopez and Scott 2000: 3)

And wisely they conclude:

> What is ... [clear] ... however, is the belief that analyses of institutional and relational structure offer *complementary*, not alternative, frameworks of sociological analysis. Sociology will prosper only if it recognizes this.
>
> (Lopez and Scott 2000: 4, emphasis in original)

At the level of substantive theory, and in contrast to the neo-institutionalists (see above, p. 121), several scholars, most notably David
Lockwood (1992), had already practically anticipated Lopez and Scott's
position and had begun to uncover the possibilities created by the forgotten conceptual legacy identified by Lopez.

In the broadest terms, and when read with a neoclassical sensibility,
Foucault too contributed to both the development of this richer concept of
structure and indeed the development of a properly sociological understanding of the nature of identity. This he did by reworking themes taken
from Durkheim and Weber against a background that owes a lot to Marx's
understanding of the nature of capitalism and the manner of its emergence
from feudalism (Trombadori 1991). More specifically, and to the present
writer at least, Foucault's concept of discourse and his appreciation of its
social significance appear to be akin to Durkheim's concept of collective
representations. Foucault's understanding of the nature of power seems to
be similarly related to Weber's concept of power. What makes Foucault's
reworking of these concepts particularly useful is: first, he rediscovers
understandings of the areas of social life to which the concepts of discourse
and power refer that had been lost as a consequence of sociology's transformation as it changed from being a largely European product to an
Atlanticist phenomenon; and second, he combines the concepts of discourse and power to produce a new understanding of the interrelationships
between the social phenomena to which the concepts of discourse, power
and identity refer.

What had been lost as Durkheim's insistence on the importance of
culture crossed the Atlantic was much sense of the complexity of the relations between the cultural and other dimensions of social life. In the hands
of Parsons, for example, the cultural realm simply took the place of the
economy in orthodox Marxism as the fundamental determinant of everything else. What had been lost as Weber's concept of power crossed the
Atlantic was any sense of power as a way of summarizing the outcome of
what is in all significant instances a complex set of interactions. Instead,
power came to be understood as some kind of substance or capability
(Hindess, 1996) or 'rules and resources' in Giddens' formulation. Weber
defined power as follows: 'the chance of a man or a number of men to
realize their own will in a communal action even against the resistance of
others'. Thus Weber understood power to be a probabalistic phenomenon
('the chance of') that summarizes the outcome of a complex set of factors and
takes the form of a relationship that is never entirely one-way ('resistance' is
part of the definition); that is, so far from power referring to a substance or
capability of some kind, it provides a shorthand way of summarizing a
complex set of relations by referring to one of its outcomes, namely the
triumph of one person's or group's will over another. Thus power is understood not as something that is distributed but as a product of a certain

disposition of social relations. In apparently unknowingly rediscovering Weber's original concept of power, Foucault also recovered a Durkheimian appreciation of the complexity of the relations between the cultural and other dimensions of the social by seeing culture as always embedded in, and contributing to, the complex sets of relations that produce power differences:

> ... 'Power', insofar as it is permanent, repetitious, inert, and self-reproducing, is simply the over-all effect that emerges from all these mobilities, the concatenation that rests on each of them and seeks in turn to arrest their movement ... power is not an institution, and not a structure; neither is it a strength we are endowed with; it is the name that one attributes to a complex strategical situation in a particular society ... Power is not something that is seized, or shared, something that one holds on to or allows to slip away; power is exercised from innumerable points, in the interplay of non-egalitarian and mobile relations.
>
> (Foucault,1979: 93–4)

Towards the end of his life, Foucault turned his attention to the study of the techniques of power, to the study of what he called 'governmentality'. When comparing liberal states to the preceding feudal and absolutist states, he noticed that the mode of governance deployed by the liberal state was much less direct in that the citizenry were not so much told what to do as instructed in how to govern themselves and administratively supported in so doing. On Nikolas Rose's (1999) highly influential reading, these techniques represented a mode of 'governing at a distance' and, shockingly to some, their deployment produced and sustained a key element in the new system of liberal governance, namely 'freedom' (cf. Durkheim's account of the development of liberty, see above, p. 51). Thus instead of freedom being the natural condition of humanity before the existence of states, as it was for John Locke and the liberal tradition, it is understood by Foucault to have been the more-or-less accidental creation of states as they gained knowledge of their populations and tried to work out how to govern them. That is, as the emergence of capitalism made it increasingly clear that labour was as important a source of national wealth as land, animals or natural resources, states sought knowledge of their populations through the gathering of stat(e)istics concerning such events as births, deaths and marriages, and such attributes as property ownership, occupation, education and health.

In this way, populations gradually gained individual identities or statuses (Marshall 1949) as persons of a certain age and gender, members of particular families, inhabitants of particular towns and villages, and property owners, craftsmen, or whatever. At the same time, on the basis of what in continental Europe was termed the science of police, the state began providing help in developing individual skills, maintaining the population's health and sanity, and securing the safety of its persons and property, all of which produced additional sets of individuating records and therefore possible knowledges. In sum, through a three-level process of observation, social support, and state record keeping, populations became both individuated and more-or-less capable of taking care of and managing themselves in a peaceable, productive and apparently self-governing way. Clearly then, here is both confirmation that Foucault should not be read as an idealist, and confirmation that he was committed to the view that social relations are the source of identities rather than vice versa.

In sum, the neoclassicists, having rejected monocausal approaches, whether Marxist or Parsonian, have found ways to combine the insights and concepts of diverse traditions in order to create a more adequate basis for understanding social structure by investigating how the relational and institutional structures that make up the economic, political and cultural/discursive dimensions of social life interact with one another in ways that are not mediated by actors, whether individual or corporate, to produce, for example, new status orders. I specifically mention the concept of status order here because this is the concept that the neoclassicists use to understand the articulation of the new cultural phenomena of concern to those committed to identity theory with those phenomena central to the social-structural problematic. The possibility of status differences, where status, as defined by Weber, refers to positive or negative estimations of social honour, means that groups may be both distinguished and arranged in a hierarchy on almost any grounds provided it is possible to think more-or-less well about a person on that basis – sadly race, ethnicity and gender all too obviously lend themselves to the making of such judgements. Moreover, when understood as an aspect of a mode of governmentality those so identified and categorized may be managed on this basis by adjusting the levels and forms of discrimination or entitlement applicable to their status group. All of which creates the somewhat disturbing possibility that the net social effect of the sociological focus on identity has not simply been to contribute to the occlusion of capitalism and its pathologies but also to have made an unwitting but major contribution to the emergence of a new form of an old mode of governance – divide and rule (for variations on this theme, see Lockwood 1992; Chatterjee 1998; Fraser 2000; Woodiwiss 2001: 64–75; Hechter 2004).

Globalization, Pacific Asia and the reappearance of social structure

Given the relative invisibility of neoclassical work, the most obvious sign to date that the concept of social structure may be about to reappear within sociological pictures of social life is the fact that it is no longer possible to talk of modernity in the singular as a universally applicable category. One must talk instead of modernities, whether multiple or alternative, in order to avoid the risk of sounding unsophisticated. Thus far the principal consequence of this has been to empty the term modernity of even what little sociological meaning it had. As indicated above (pp. 110–11), if modernity means anything at all sociologically, it refers to a society that either places the individual at the centre of its value system or, more substantively, shares many of its social-structural features with the United States. Currently, the recognition of the social differences between the United States and Asian societies is generally limited to an acknowlegement that Asian values are not those of individualism with the result that, if the existence of an Asian modernity is allowed, the core element supposedly distinguishing it as a social condition can no longer apply, which leaves the term modernity simply meaning 'society as it is nowadays'.

To me this suggests that, in the absence of any viable alternative, the concept of modernity should be rejected altogether and that of capitalism restored, because this promises to allow a deeper understanding of the differences between Asian and Western societies. The one proviso is that the concept of capitalism deployed should not be an economically determinist one. Thus, using Lopez and Scott's vocabulary, although the establishment and maintenance of capitalist economic relations depends on certain broad economic, legal and political requirements in terms of environing sets of invisible *social relations* being met, it is essential to understand that these generic requirements may be met in many and very different *institutional* and therefore visible ways. Indeed this is one of the most important lessons that neoclassical sociologists such as myself have derived from our encounters with Asia. Capitalism as a system of economic relations is undoubtedly well established in Asia, which means that it must be nested in broadly supportive sets of economic, political and cultural relations. However, many of the more specific values and institutions commonly considered either to be necessary prerequisites for, or to follow necessarily from, the presence of a capitalist economy, like an individualist ideology, the rule of law, and liberal democracy, were neither present in advance of the arrival of capitalist economic relations nor subsequently established (Woodiwiss 1990c).

The broader requirements upon which the establishment and survival of capitalist economic relations depend are the following: an economy premissed upon the private possession of property in the means of production, and the existence of more or less free markets in land, labour, raw materials, and the commodities produced by enterprises; a state possessing a monopoly of legitimate force within its territory and protective of private property; a cultural and especially a legal system that legitimizes capital's appropriation of any economic surplus as a profit whose disposition is left largely to the discretion of the owner of the enterprise. In the case of the United States, these requirements are met in the following ways. Economically, virtually all property in the means of production is privately owned and markets are more-or-less competitive and minimally regulated. Insofar as there is economic coordination, it takes the form of the private ordering created by oligopolies in certain markets and is therefore simply the product of market power. Any such coordination is also necessarily informal, because most forms of non-market, inter-firm coordination are illegal as a consequence of anti-trust legislation. Politically, the state is strongly protective of private property, liberal-democratic in form, and intervenes minimally in the management of social and economic relations. In addition, although the constitutional right to bear arms means that the state does not possess an absolute monopoly of legitimate force, it seems reasonable to say that in practice it does possess such a monopoly, because the state determines the conditions under which individuals can legitimately use their weapons. Culturally, the core values are markedly individualistic, and legally too the protection of individual freedom, especially as it relates to property ownership, defines the content of core doctrines.

In Pacific Asia, the general relational requirements are met in very different institutional ways. Economically, while private ownership of property in the means of production is widespread, it often coexists with state ownership of such resources, whether they be land as in China, Hong Kong and Singapore or industrial enterprises and utilities as in China. Again, while markets are broadly free, states often impose restrictions on who can own natural resources, as in the Philippines, and even take up certain jobs, as in Malaysia where certain occupations are reserved for ethnic Malays. While acknowledging the significant variations in the way this is achieved in individual countries, the high level of privately organized economic coordination that is characteristic of Pacific-Asian societies (Whitely 1992: Chapter 3) represents a striking difference in economic organization as compared to the United States (see Figure 9.1). Thus Japan's economy is largely organized through the huge, shareholder-owned industrial/financial combines known as *keiretsu*, South Korea's by the equally huge but often still family-owned and state-supported industrial/financial combines known as *chaebol*, and in the remainder of the region similar levels of coordination are achieved through the networks of 'Chinese family businesses' (Clegg and Redding 1990; Shieh 1992; Whitely 1992).

Politically, most states in the region, apart from those with significant insurgencies such as the Philippines and Indonesia, possess a monopoly of legitimate force and are sometimes liberal democratic and sometimes not.

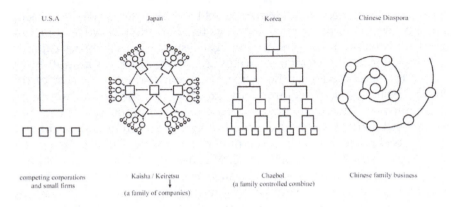

Figure 9.1 Comparative business systems

Although states are broadly supportive of private property, they are also often energetically interventionist and tend to give what are commonly termed 'national' goals and interests precedence over private goals and interests. Thus many of them have created new industries, restricted outward flows of investment resources, subsidized research and development, protected their home markets, provided overseas market intelligence free to private companies, and made massive investments in such elements of social infrastructure as housing and education (Appelbaum and Henderson 1992: 21–2).

Culturally, the core discourses of rule are typically hybrids comprising elements of familialism, individualism and social democracy, with the result that an owner's entitlement to dispose of any economic surplus is strongly reinforced by expectations of benevolence on the owner's part and of loyalty and filial piety on the part of employees; that is, superior levels of income and wealth are justified not simply by reference to talent or risk-taking but also by reference to the successful discharge of obligations owed to other members of the pertinent group.[1] What this means in terms of a practical discourse of political rule has been well put in relation to South East Asia, for example, by David Jones:

> we can broadly identify a number of what might be termed shared values that significantly shape political and economic development ... 'Consensus', as modernized Asian politicians describe the traditional pursuit of balance, does not require a pluralistic consultation of a multiplicity of interests, far less submission to popular taste. Politically, East Asian political thought of a Confucian provenance asserted the need for hierarchy and expertise. Rule was always the responsibility of a virtuous elite or a man of prowess. In a Confucian tradition it was the self-cultivated *jinzi* who rectified

the people, whilst in Southeast Asia, with its blend of Hindu, Islamic and Buddhist political-theocratic understandings, indirect consultation enabled rule to proceed by apparent agreement, or *gotong royong*. In its modern version, the professional expert replaces the *jinzi* and technocratically adjusts the people to their required role. Harmony is still valued and achieved, not by a proliferation of interests, but by each member precisely fulfilling an ordained relationship, or, in Southeast Asia, by subtly deferring to the requirements of respectful consensus building (*musyawarah maafekat*).

(Jones 1998: 55; see also, Woodiwiss 1998)

Although Western law has long been embedded in Pacific-Asian societies, whether as a result of colonialism as in much of South East Asia, under duress as in such non-colonized societies as Japan and South Korea (Seizlet 1992), or because of the rules of the World Trade Organization as in the case of China today, it too has taken on a distinctly local colouration in that it is typically strongly marked by familialism (Woodiwiss 1998, 2003). The most striking result of this is that the law plays a far less important role in Asian social life than it does in that of the West. This is because the pervasive familialism leads to a strong preference for private, extra-legal mediation or conciliation as opposed to public court hearings because the latter can result in all parties to a case losing face and so interfere with other valued long-term relationships.

In sum, when Pacific-Asian societies are looked at in terms of the problematic of social structure rather than that of identity, it is clear that their differences as compared to the United States are not simply matters of culture but comprehensive. In other words, Pacific-Asian societies are not to be understood as hybrid because they combine Eastern cultures with Western economic and political institutions, but as hybrid all the way down, so to speak. Although this has yet to be reflected in much of the pertinent literature, this in turn means that Pacific-Asian societies are also different as regards their class and status dynamics. This is because the latter are the interactive effects of economic, political and ideological/discursive relations (for accounts of these dynamics in a number of Pacific-Asian societies, see Woodiwiss 1992, 1998). All this leads to the conclusion that, contrary to the expectations of modernization theorists, Asian societies are most unlikely to become anything at all close to simulacra of the United States, or even Western Europe for that matter. Rather they will remain markedly different and very likely become increasingly influential alternative models of social organization, not least because China seems to be well on the way to replicating in the twenty-first century Japan's establishment of a non-liberal capitalist society in the nineteenth century.

Conclusion

In this chapter I have developed my argument by contrasting Asia in general or Pacific Asia more particularly, with the United States and only occasionally with the broader category of the West which would include Western Europe. This is not only because the Atlanticist social theory I am criticizing is an American-led discourse, but also because the contrast between Pacific Asia and Europe is much less marked than that between Pacific Asia and the United States. Despite Europe being the home of liberalism and the institutional arrangements it validates, European capitalisms are much more like their Pacific-Asian than their American equivalents. Indeed, European Christian- and social-democratic ideas have been a major source of inspiration as regards economic and social policy in Pacific Asia. Thanks to the ending of the Cold War and to the extremism of the present American administration, the differences between Western Europe and the United States have become much easier for non-specialists to see and indeed, in an unparalleled fashion, these differences have become a topic for public debate in Europe. Not the least of the reasons for this interest are the divergent responses to the present state of the world that these differences have produced:

> Americans, and especially the Bush administration and its supporters, believe that US primacy is the defining feature of the contemporary world ... Or, as the opening sentence of the Bush Administration's National Security Strategy put it: 'The United States possesses unprecedented – unequalled – strength and influence in the world,' which it should use 'to promote a balance of power that favors freedom.' Europeans, in contrast, tend to see globalization – including the constraints it places on any one nation's power – as the defining feature of the current era ... The sheer speed and volume of cross-border contacts and the fact that globalization is occurring across multiple dimensions simultaneously mean that neither its positive nor its negative consequences can be managed by individual countries on their own. As a consequence, whether the issue is terrorism, organized crime, weapons proliferation, infectious diseases, democratization, or trade in goods and services, no one country – not even the most powerful – can secure its goals without the aid of others.
>
> (Daalder 2003: 151–2)

If, to use Robert Kagan's (2003) memorable formulation, 'Europeans are from Venus and Americans from Mars', the questions that arise are: 'What might be the significance of such differences for Atlanticist social theory?' and 'Might Atlanticist sociology one day be replaced by a more authentically cosmopolitan social theory?' The answers to these questions will depend to a significant degree on how the next generation of social scientists exercise their theoretical freedom and fulfil their reflexive responsibilities. In the meantime, it would be very instructive for the reader to compare the story that has just been told with the version of the same story told by the American theorist Jeffrey Alexander (2003: Chapter 8). Despite many similarities in both our analytical approaches and the structure and content of our narratives, Alexander problematizes neither the utility of the concept of modernity nor the centrality of the concepts of identity and culture. Unsurprisingly, therefore, he predicts the imminent arrival of a neo-modernizationist theory as the successor to postmodernism for what are otherwise many of the same reasons that I predict the final demise of the Atlanticism that contributed to the initial formation of modernization theory.

Note

1   For Weber, familialism or patriarchalism was the elementary form of traditional authority and is defined as follows:

> [It] is the situation where, within a group (household) which is usually organized on both an economic and kinship basis, a particular individual governs who is designated by a definite rule of inheritance. The decisive characteristic ... is the belief of the members that domination, even though it is an inherent traditional right of the master, must definitely be exercized as a joint right in the interests of all members and is thus not freely appropriated by the incumbent. In order that this shall be maintained, it is crucial that in both cases there is a complete absence of a personal (patrimonial) staff. Hence the master is still largely dependent upon the willingness of the members to comply with his orders since he has no machinery to enforce them. Therefore the members are not yet really subjects.
>
> (Weber 1968: 231)

For Weber, then, patriarchalism was a strictly hierarchical political structure justified by a familialist discourse and resting on an economy and a wider set of social relations structured in large part by kinship. For a discussion of the nature and variety of familialist discourses of rule and the conditions under which they may retain legitimacy where states exist and capitalism has displaced kinship-based economic relations, see Woodiwiss 1998, 2003: Chapter 4).

Conclusion: in praise of the *ateliers* of sociology

I have tried to do two things in this book. The first is to introduce the modes of theorizing most likely to be encountered by those wishing to read, use or produce social theory. The second is to demonstrate how to go about making at least one kind of theoretical intervention. As regards the first task, I have shown how different combinations of ontological assumptions concerning the nature of the social and epistemological assumptions concerning how to produce knowledge or pictures of social life result in different research strategies and therefore different modes of theory construction. In a sense, knowledge of the five different metatheoretical positions that I have identified constitutes the secret knowledge of sociology and the other disciplines that have social theory as their core. I use the term 'secret knowledge' not so much because few people have access to knowledge of metatheory, as because of the problem created by the fact that many practitioners and theorists are not explicit about, and sometimes not even aware of, their metatheoretical assumptions. Thus, given that identifying these assumptions is the key to understanding any sociological or sociologically related work whether of a theoretical or a substantive kind, the question that arises is 'How can one discover that about which the author is silent?' To summarize the argument provided in this book, my answer is to suggest that we follow Durkheim and, just as he had to find a 'visible index' when he was trying to convince his readers that there had been dramatic changes in the nature of social solidarity over time, seek out an index from which we can read off the nature of any undeclared metatheoretical assumptions.

As I have shown in Part One, such assumptions are important because they explain why theorists work where they do, deploy certain methods and not others, and define their concepts in the ways they do. What I mean by the last point is that what visibly distinguishes different types of theory from one another is that they define their concepts by referring to particular orders of being and/or particular visible aspects of whatever may be the object of concern; that is, they exhibit what might be called different styles of definition. Thus, for example, empiricists define classes as strata of people delimited as visible bands of income levels or clusters of occupations, whilst realists (in this case Marxists) define classes by reference to the visible inequalities produced by otherwise invisible sets of production relations, and interpretivists (in this case Weberians) define classes as groups of people whose visible actions demonstrate that they are conscious of the relationship between their structural positions, however understood, and their life chances. In sum, it is the differences between their metatheoretical assumptions that explains why empiricists define classes by reference to income or occupation, whereas Marxists define them by reference to inequalities, and Weberians by reference to actions.

Workplaces, methodological choices and styles of conceptualization, then, are all products of metatheoretical commitments, and therefore they may also serve as rough-and-ready but reasonably reliable visible indices of such commitments (see above p. 80 for some caveats). In other words, looking behind the conceptual language deployed, which itself of course also contains many clues, it should be possible to read back from the sites on which it was produced, the methods used, and the style of conceptualization to uncover a text's otherwise implicit metatheoretical assumptions. Thus knowledge of metatheory constitutes a secret knowledge because it can uncover things about a text that even the author her or himself may not know. This, of course, is important because it enhances the understanding of what is being read. But it is perhaps even more important because the combination of being able to identify the metatheoretical assumptions of others with a knowledge of your own assumptions is the key to being able to engage in sustained critical and creative dialogue with the existing body of sociological and related work. In saying this, I am assuming, as I have done throughout, that a social scientist has to base his or her work on a single metatheoretical position. This is because, otherwise, serious issues are likely to arise concerning the coherence of his or her reasoning. Thus, for example, we cannot simultaneously believe that society depends upon us thinking about it for its existence and does not so depend, or is both accessible and not accessible through our senses. Many have tried and they have all failed in that they have ended up following one of the positions at the expense of the other, as I have indicated with respect to Weber, Lukacs, Parsons, and Giddens. However, the question still remains as to how the nature of the relationship between the knowledges produced on the basis of the different sets of assumptions should be understood. The difficulty is, again, that although they are all valid on their own terms, these terms themselves are mutually exclusive. Thus, if the veracity of any particular set of knowledge claims is accepted, the veracity of the others cannot logically be accepted. This said, the important point to be recognized is that the simultaneous existence of such different knowledges is the product of social forces rather than of purely individual reasoning. Consequently, these knowledges may best be understood, despite their incommensurability, as being related to one another through being mutually available as sources of insight and inspiration, or indeed questions and challenges.

Whatever tradition a social scientist works within, a capacity for critical thinking is essential if he or she wishes to engage in theorizing because it is typically by discovering either inconsistencies or gaps in, and/or limits to, existing theories that a point of entry into the always ongoing work of theory making can be found. At the most basic level, once the metatheoretical assumptions informing the text or texts being considered have been established, they can be compared with one's own prefered set of assumptions. Any differences can serve as the beginnings of a critical engagement with the texts being assessed, because the reasons one has for one's own preferences are not likely to be acknowledged or appreciated by those who work on the basis of different assumptions.

In general terms, there are two major forms of potentially productive critical activity: internal critique and external critique. Internal critique is usually produced by those who either share, or for critical purposes temporarily take up, the assumptions of the texts they are considering, and it is largely confined either to finding inconsistencies and/or gaps in an existing theory and its accompanying body of evidence, or to exposing a theory's limits in terms of what it does or does not explain (see the accounts of the contributions by Lukacs, Gramsci, and Althusser to the theorization of the power/knowledge relation in Chapter 6). Internal critique seldom results in radical changes to theories and is therefore most often regarded as a means of developing the theory concerned.

External critique, on the other hand, almost always aspires to achieve just such radical changes (see the accounts of the contributions of Saussure and Foucault to the theorization of the power/knowledge relation in Chapter 6 and indeed Part 2 of the present text). Thus, although it is often initially prompted by, say, an unhappiness with the social consequences of a particular way of looking at the world, as in Marx's case, the constructive side of critical activity typically begins by fastening on to the problems uncovered by internal critiques and, as with Kuhn's paradigm changes, arguing that there is a better way to look at whatever it is that the criticized theory is being used to understand. In sociology and related disciplines, which are assertively multiparadigmatic, the critical difference usually turns out to be a matter of metatheory, as is illustrated by Marx's *Theses on Feuerbach* and the way in which I establish the starting point of my argument for a change in the meaning and practice of reflexivity. Sometimes the inconsistencies, gaps, and limits uncovered by internal critique are of a logical kind, but most often they are of a substantive kind. Thus, at least in the realist tradition, a problem is not solved by simply identifying it and changing the definitions of the pertinent concepts. This is because the missing conceptual pieces and the supporting evidence also have to be provided and shown to produce a superior account of both the old and the new evidence. Hence my resorting to Saussure and Foucault's concepts and what might otherwise seem to be the self-aggrandizing references to my own more substantive work on the United States and Asia in my argument for a change in the meaning and practice of reflexivity.

I will now turn to the second of the tasks set for this book. Although it is probably quixotic, far from adequately developed or empirically supported, and indeed could now I hope be strongly challenged by any reasonably attentive reader of this book, my argument for a transformation in the nature of sociological reflexivity is not simply something dreamt up for illustrative purposes. Assuming then, for arguments sake, that I have made my case, what conclusions might be drawn from it?

First, the recent past has seen a pronounced weakening of social theory because far too many concepts – social structure, class, status, ideology, and even discursive formation, for example – have been forgotten. As reflected in the fact that all the term modernity actually means is 'now', the present is no longer thought to have a history.

Second, if such naive presentism is to be reversed and avoided in the future, practitioners, and perhaps especially those with a special interest in theory should be more vigilant with respect to unwanted influences from the wider society that can lead to such overreactions. Bourdieu, as ever, has described what this involves very concretely:

> To avoid becoming the object of the problems that you take as your object, you must retrace the history of the emergence of these problems, of their progressive constitution, i.e., of the collective work, often times accomplished though competition and struggle, that proved necessary to make such and such issues to be known and recognized as legitimate problems, problems that are avowable, publishable, public, official ... In all these cases ... the problem that ordinary positivism (which is the first inclination of every researcher) takes for granted has been socially produced, in and by a collective work of construction of social reality and that it took meetings and committees, associations and leagues, caucuses and movements, demonstrations and petition drives, demands and deliberations, votes and stands, projects, programs, and resolutions to cause what was and could have remained a private, particular, singular problem to turn into a social problem, a public issue that can be publicly addressed (think of the fate of abortion or homosexuality) or even an official problem that becomes the object of official decisions and policies, of laws and decrees.
>
> (Bourdieu and Wacquant 1992: 238–9)

Third, notwithstanding all of the above, and more positively, practitioners are not totally at the mercy of the discursive formations that define the terrain within which they work, since they can make a difference with respect to enunciative modalities, concepts and strategies (the appearance of every new theory demonstrates this). This possibility, however, demarcates not only their areas of freedom and resistance but also their area of responsibility and their opportunity for virtue. That is, they are free, and indeed have the responsibility to make their own judgements in these areas rather than allow them to be made by external forces, whether thanks to old commitments or new opportunities. Sadly, little advantage was taken of this freedom and less attention paid to its accompanying intellectual responsibilities during the final 20 or so years of the twentieth century. This said, it is equally true that the likely effectiveness of any exercise of theoretical responsibility is very uncertain. This is because of the varying functionalities of particular discourses in the fields of non-discursive practice and desire. For, as everyone knows, desire tends to attach itself to novelty rather than to what the impressively stoical American socialist writer, Irving Howe (1996), has called 'steady work'. And sometimes it is simply the case that nobody is listening – a state of affairs that is hardly surprising because steady work necessarily means from time to time continuing to take an interest in things, places, or ideas that most people have lost interest in, that have become marginal. Under such circumstances virtue, as ever, must be its own reward.

From what has been said and argued in this book, I hope it is clear that producing social theory is a craft that requires both a continuous alternation between abstract and empirical work and the cooperative efforts of the female as well as male equivalents of the diversely skilled masters, journeymen, and apprentices who worked in the craft workshops that used to populate the Clerkenwell district of London where I work. These equivalents are the variously skilled and theoretically diverse academics, graduate and undergraduate students that people university departments. And where departments work well they do indeed exhibit the solidaristic ethos (Sutton 1994) and secret knowledges, as well as the idiosyncracies and indeed the 'novelistic side' of the old craft workshops. I end on this point because it sometimes seems that such departments are considered hopelessly old-fashioned by those who occupy the commanding heights of the power/knowledge complex and who appear to think that social science departments should be simply teaching units whilst research is carried out in specialized centres and knowledge corporations. Such a separation of roles might possibly work in some natural science disciplines where intellectual diversity is perhaps not quite so critical. However, it would be fatal for the disciplines that have social theory as their core and where such diversity and the accompanying secret knowledge are vital both for the nurturing of new talent and the sustaining of more mature talents through the continuous challenges that arise as a result of working alongside people with very different positions. In sum, sociologists and their kin have a problem and those who value their disciplines with their special freedoms and responsibilities need to find a way to communicate, not least to themselves, what is desirable about their current working arrangements. The term 'department' does not do it, nor does the term workshop. The term *atelier*, on the other hand, connotes just such a desirable setting, not least because it is french and is currently used mainly to refer to the design studios/workshops of *haute couture* fashion houses, which, because of the close proximity of the drawing boards and cutting tables, are the last redoubt of true innovation in the clothing industry. So perhaps, then, re-imagining departments as *ateliers* would do the trick? Minimally, we might start to dress better – present company excepted, of course.

References

Abrams, P. (1968) *The Origins of British Sociology, 1834–1914* Chicago: University of Chicago Press.

Abercrombie, N., Hill, S. and Turner, B.S. (eds) (1990) *Dominant Ideologies.* London: Unwin Hyman.

Aglietta, M. (1976) *The Theory of Capitalist Regulation,* London: Verso.

Alexander, J. (2003) *The Meanings of Social Life.* New York: Oxford University Press.

Alpers, S. (1983) *The Art of Describing: Dutch Art in the Seventeenth Century.* Chicago: University of Chigago Press.

Althusser, L. (1969) *For Marx.* London: Allen Lane.

Althusser, L. (1971) *Lenin and Philosophy.* London: New Left Books.

Amadae, S. (2003) *Rationalizing Capitalist Democracy: the Cold War Origins of Rational Choice Liberalism.* Chicago: University of Chicago Press.

Anderson, P. (1992) *The Peculiarities of the English.* London: Verso.

Appelbaum, R. and Henderson, J. (eds) (1992) *States and Development in the Asian Pacific Rim.* London: Sage.

Apter, D. (1965) *The Politics of Modernization.* Chicago: University of Chicago Press.

Archer, M., Collier, A. and Porpora, D. (2004) *Transcendence: Critical Realism and God.* London: Routledge.

Bannister, R.C. (1991) *Sociology and Scientism: the American Quest for Objectivity, 1880–1940.* Chapel Hill: University of North Carolina Press.

Barthes, R. (1977) *Roland Barthes.* Basingstoke: Macmillan.

Baudrillard, J. (1995) *Simulacra and Simulation.* Ann Arbor: University of Michigan Press.

Bauman, Z. (2004) *Identity.* Cambridge: Polity.

Beck, U., Giddens, A. and Lash, S. (1994) *Reflexive Modernization.* Oxford: Polity.

Bell, C. and Newby, H. (eds) (1977) *Doing Sociological Research.* New York: Free Press.

Bell, D. (1960) *The End of Ideology*. Cambridge: Harvard University Press.

Bell, D. (1967) *Marxian Socialism in the United States*. Princeton: Princeton University Press.

Bell. D. (1973) *The Coming of Postindustrial Society*. New York: Basic Books.

Bell, D. (1976) *The Cultural Contradictions of Capitalism*. New York: Basic Books.

Benjamin, W. (1977) *The Origins of German Tragic Drama*. London: Verso.

Benton, E. (1977) *The Philosophical Foundations of the Three Sociologies*, London: Routledge.

Benton, E. (1984) *The Rise of Structuralist Marxism*. London: Macmillan.

Berger, J. and Zelditch, M. (eds) (2002) *New Directions in Contemporary Sociological Theory*. Lanham: Rowman & Littlefield.

Berger J., Wagner, D.G. and Zelditch, M. Jr (1989) Theory growth, social processes and metatheory, in Turner, D. (ed.) *Theory Building in Sociology: Assessing Theoretical Cumulation*. Newbury Park CA: Sage.

Berger, P. (1967) *A Rumour of Angels*. New York, Anchor.

Bhabha, H. (1994) *The Location of Culture*. London: Routledge.

Bhaskar, R. (1978) *A Realist Theory of Science*. Brighton: Harvester.

Bhaskar, R. (1986) *Scientific Realism and Human Emancipation*. London: Verso.

Bhaskar, R. (1989), *Reclaiming Reality*. London: Verso.

Bhaskar, R. (2000) *From East to West: Odyssey of a Soul*. London: Routledge.

Blalock, H. (1994) Why have we failed to systematize reality's complexity, in Hage (1994).

Bottero, W. (2004) Class identities and the identity of class, *Sociology*, 38(5): 985–1004.

Bourdieu, P. and Nice, R. (1984) *Distinction: a social critique of the judgment of taste*. Cambridge: Harvard University Press.

Bourdieu, P. and Wacquant, L. (1992) *An Invitation to Reflexive Sociology*. Chicaco: University of Chicago Press.

Bourdieu, P. and Wacquant, L. (1999) On the cunning of imperialist reason, *Theory, Culture and Society*, 16(1): 41–58.

Bradbury, M. and McFarlane, J. (1991) *Modernism: 1890–1930*. Harmondsworth: Penguin.

Braverman, H. (1974) *Labor and Monopoly Capitalism*. New York: Monthly Review Press.

Brick, H. (1986) *Daniel Bell and the Decline of Intellectual Radicalism: Social Theory and Political Reconciliation in the 1940s*. Madison: University of Wisconsin Press.

Bryman, A. (2004) *Social Research Methods*. Oxford: Oxford University Press.

Buci-Glucksman, C. (1994) *Baroque Reason*. London: Sage.

Burchell, G., Gordon, C. and Miller, P. (eds) (1991) *The Foucault Effect: Studies in Governmentality*. London: Harvester.

Callinicos, A. (1989) *Against Postmodernism: a marxist critique*. Cambridge: Polity.

Callinicos, A. and Harman, C. (1987) *The Changing Working Class*. London: Bookmarks.

Carver, T. (1975) *Texts on Method: Karl Marx*. Oxford: Blackwell.

Chatterjee, P. (1998) Community in the East, *Economic and Political Weekly*, 7 February, pp. 277–82.

Clegg, S. and Redding, S. (eds) (1990) *The Enterprise and Management in East Asia*. Hong Kong: Centre for Asian Studies, University of Hong Kong.

Coleman, J. (1990) *Foundations of Social Theory*. Cambridge MA: Harvard University Press.

Collins, R. (1998) *The Sociology of Philosophies*. Cambridge MA: Harvard University Press.

Commission on the Social Sciences (2003) *Great Expectations: the social sciences in Britain*. London: Commission on the Social Sciences.

Craib, I (1998) *Experiencing Identity*. London: Sage.

Crewe, I (1986) The death and resurrection of class voting, *Political Studies*, xxxiv: 4.

Crompton, R., Devine, F., Savage, M. and Scott, J. (eds) (2000) *Renewing Class Analysis*. Oxford: Blackwell.

Daalder, I. (2003) The end of Atlanticism, *Survival*, 45(2): 147–66.

Davis, M. (1986) *Prisoners of the American Dream*. London: Verso.

Derrida, J. (1977) *Of Grammatology*. Johns Hopkins University Press, Baltimore.

Devine, F. (1998) Social identities, class identity and political perspectives, *Sociological Review*, 40(2): 229–52.

Devine, F. and Savage, M. (2000) Conclusion: renewing class analysis, in Crompton, *et al.* (2000).

Durkheim, E. (1995) *The Elementary Forms of Religious Life*. New York: The Free Press.

Durkheim, E. (1997a) *The Division of Labour*. New York: The Free Press.

Durkheim, E. (1997b) *Suicide*. New York: The Free Press.

Durkheim, E. (1988) *The Rules of Sociological Method*. Basingstoke: Macmillan.

Fanon, F. (1967) *Black Skin White Mask*. Translated and republished in 1991. New York: Grove Press.

Featherstone, M. (ed.) (1990) *Global Culture: Nationalism, Globalization and Culture*. London: Sage.

Foster, H. (ed.) (1988) *Vision and Visuality*. Seattle: Bay Press.

Foucault, M. (1972) *The Archaeology of Knowledge*. London: Tavistock.

Foucault, M. (1979) *The History of Sexuality*, vol. 1. Penguin: Harmondsworth.

Frank, D. and Meyer, D. (2000) The contemporary identity explosion: individualizing society in the post-war period: Mimeo, Harvard University, Cambridge MA.

Frank, T. (2000) *One Market under God: Extreme Capitalism, Market Populism and the End of Economic Democracy*. New York: Doubleday.

Frank, T. (2005) *What's the matter with Kansas: How Conservatives Won the Heart of America*, 2nd edn. New York: Metropolitan Books.

Fraser, N. (2000) Rethinking recognition, *New Left Review*, 3: 107–20.

Friedan, B. (1963) *The Feminine Mystique*. New York: Dell.

Friedland, R. and Mohr, J. (2004) *Matters of Culture: Cultural Sociology in Practice*. New York: Cambridge University Press.

Gane, M. (1988) *On Durkheim's Rules of Sociological Method*. London: Routledge.

Gergen, K. (2000) *The Saturated Self*. New York: Basic Books.

Gerth, H. and Mills, C.W. (1948) *From Max Weber*. London: Routledge.

Giddens, A. (1984) *The Constitution of Society*. Cambridge: Polity.

Giddens, A. (1990) *The Consequences of Modernity*. Stanford: Stanford University Press.

Giddens, A. (1991) *Modernity and Self-Identity*. Stanford: Stanford University Press.

Gilman, N. (2004) *Mandarins of the Future: Modernization Theory in Cold War America*. Baltimore: Johns Hopkins University Press.

Gluck, C. (1985) *Japan's Modern Myths: Ideology in the Late Meiji Period*. Princeton: Princeton University Press.

Goldthorpe, J. (1980) *Social Mobility and Class Structure in Modern Britain*. Oxford: Oxford University Press.

Goldthorpe, J., Lockwood, D., Bechhofer, F. and Platt, J. (1969) *The Affluent Worker*, 3 vols. Cambridge: Cambridge University Press.

Gramsci, A. (1971) *Selections from the Prison Notebooks*. New York: International Publishers.

Gregg, P., Wadsworth, J. and Dickens, R. (eds) (2003) *The Labour Market under New Labour*. Basingstoke: Palgrave Macmillan.

Hage, J. (ed.) (1994) *Formal Theory in Sociology: Opportunity or Pitfall?* Albany: State University of New York Press.

Halberg, M. (1989) Feminist Epistemology: an impossible project, *Radical Philosophy*, 53: 3–7.

Hall, S. (1988) *The Hard Road to Renewal: Thatcherism and the Crisis of the Left*. London: Verso.

Hall, S. and Jacques, M. (1985) *The Politics of Thatcherism*. London: Lawrence & Wishart.

Halliday, F. (1994) *Rethinking International Relations*. Basingstoke: Macmillan.

Hammond, P. (ed.) (1964) *Sociologists at Work*. New York: Harper Collins.

Harding, S. (1986) *The Science Question in Feminism*. New York: Cornell University Press.

Hardt, A. and Negri, T. (2001) *Empire*. Cambridge: Harvard University Press.

Hechter, M. (2004) From class to culture, *American Journal of Sociology*, 110(2): 400–45.

Heller, T., Sosna, M. and Wellbery, T. (1986) *Reconstructing Individualism*. Stanford: Stanford University.

Henderson, D.F. (1974) 'Contracts' in Tokugawa Japan, *The Journal of Japanese Studies*. 1(1): 51.

Hindess, B. (1996) *Discourses of Power: from Hobbes to Foucault*. Oxford: Blackwell.

Hindess, B. and Hirst P. (1975) *Pre-Capitalist Modes of Production*. London: Routledge.

Hirschmeier, J. and Yui, T. (1981) *The Development of Japanese Business*. London: Allen & Unwin.

Hirst, P. (1975) *Durkheim, Bernard and Epistemology*. London: Routledge & Kegan Paul.

Hirst, P. and Thompson, G. (1999) *Globalisation in Question*, 2nd. edn. Cambridge: Polity.

Hobsbawm, E. (2005) In defence of history, *Guardian*, 15 January.

Hollier, D. (ed.) (1988) *The College of Sociology: 1937–39*. Minneapolis: University of Minnesota Press.

Holmwood, J. (1996) *Founding Sociology: Talcott Parsons and the Idea of General Sociology*. London: Longman.

Holmwood, J. and Stewart, A. (1993) *Explanation and Social Theory*. Basingstoke: Palgrave Macmillan.

Hoover, K. and Donovan, T. (2004) *The Elements of Social Scientific Theorizing*, 8th edn. Belmont: Wadsworth.

Howe, I. (1996) *Steady Work: Essays in the Politics of Democratic Radicalism, 1953–1966*. New York: Harvest Books.

Hume, D. [1779] (1990) *Dialogues Concerning Natural Religion*. Harmondsworth: Penguin.

Huntington, S. (1982) *American Politics: the Promise of Disharmony*, Cambridge: Harvard University Press.

Huntington, S. (1997) *The Clash of Civilizations and the Remaking of the World Order*. New York: Simon & Schuster.

Huysmans, J.K. (1998) *Against Nature*. Oxford: Oxford University Press.

Jameson, F. (1991) *Postmodernism or the Cultural Logic of Late Capitalism*. Durham, NC: Duke University Press.

Jay, M. (1993) *Downcast Eyes: the Denigration of Vision in Twentieth Century French Thought*. Berkeley: University of California Press.

Jay, M. (2004) *Songs of Experience*. Berkeley: University of California Press.

Jenkins, R. (1996) *Social Identity*. London: Routledge.

Jepperson, R. (2002) The development and application of neo-instutional-ism, in Berger and Zelditch (2002).

Jessop, B. (1980) *The Capitalist State: Marxist Theories and Methods*. New York: New York University Press.

Jessop, B. (2003) *The Future of the Capitalist State*. Cambridge: Polity.

Jones, D. (1998) *Political Development in Pacific Asia*. Cambridge: Polity.

Kagan, R. (2003) *Of Paradise and Power*. New York: Knopf.

Keat, R. and Urry, J. (1975) *Social Theory as Science*. London: Routledge.

Kuhn, T. (1970) *The Structure of Scientific Revolutions*. Chicago: University of Chicago Press.

Kymlicka, B. and Matthews, J. (eds) (1988) *The Reagan Revolution*. Chicago: The Dorsey Press.

Larrain, J. (1979) *Marxism and Ideology*. Basingstoke: Macmillan.

Larrain, J. (1994) The postmodern critique of ideology, *Sociological Review*. 42(2): 289–314.

Lasch, C. (1978) *The Culture of Narcissism*. New York: Norton.

Latour, B. (1993) *We Have Never Been Modern*. Cambridge: Harvard University Press.

Lee, R. (2004) Recording technologies and the interview in sociology, 1920–2000, *Sociology*, 38(5): 869–89.

Lemert, C. (2004) *Sociology: after the crisis*. Boulder: Paradigm Publishers.

Levin, D.M. (ed.) (1993) *Modernity and the Hegemony of Vision*. Berkeley: University of California Press.

Levi-Strauss, C. (1961) *Triste Tropique (A World on the Wane)*. New York: Criterion Books.

Levy, M. (1949) *Family Development in Modern China*. Cambridge MA: Harvard University Press.

Lipetz, A. (1985) *The Enchanted World*. London: Verso.

Lockwood, D. (1958) *The Blackcoated Worker*. Oxford: Oxford University Press.

Lockwood, D. (1992) *Solidarity and Schism: 'The Problem of Disorder' in Durkheimian and Marxist Sociology*. Oxford: Clarendon Press.

Lopez, J. (2003) *Society and its Metaphors*. Continuum, London.

Lopez, J. and Scott, J. (2000) *Social Structure*. Buckingham: Open University Press.

Lukacs, G. (1922) *History and Class Consciousness*. Translated and repub-lished in 1968. London: Merlin Press.

Lukes, S. (1973) *Emile Durkheim: His Life and Work*. New York: Harper Row.

Lyotard, J.F. (1979) *The Postmodern Condition*. Manchester: Manchester University Press.

Mann, M. (1986) *The Sources of Social Power*, vol. 1. Cambridge: Cambridge University Press.

Mao Tse Tung (1966) *Four Essays on Philosophy*. Beijing: Foreign Languages Press.

Maravall, J.A. (1986) *The Culture of the Baroque: Analysis of an Historical Structure*. Minneapolis: University of Minnesota Press.

Marsden, R. (1999) *The Nature of Capital: Marx after Foucault*. London: Routledge.

Marshall, G., Rose, D., Newby, H. and Vogler, C. (1989) *Social Class in Modern Britain*. London: Unwin Hyman.

Marshall, T.H. (1994) Citizenship and social class, in Turner and Hamilton (1994).

Marx, K. (1964a) *Capital*, vol. 1. London: Lawrence & Wishart.

Marx, K. (1964b) *The Economic and Philosophical Manuscripts of 1844*. New York: International Publishers.

Marx, K. (1973) *Grundrisse: Introduction to the Critique of Political Economy*. Harmondsworth: Penguin.

Marx, K. and Engels, F. (1967) *The Communist Manifesto*. Harmondsworth: Penguin.

Marx, K. and Engels, F. (1970) *The German Ideology*. London: Lawrence & Wishart.

McGinn, C. (2001) *The Making of a Philosopher*. London: Scribner.

McLennan, D. (1996) *Karl Marx*. Basingstoke: Palgrave Macmillan.

Merton, R.K. (1968) *Social Theory and Social Structure*. New York: Free Press.

Meyer, J. (1986) Myths of socialization and personality, in Heller *et al.* (1986).

Mills, C.W. (1951) *White Collar*. New York: Oxford University Press.

Mitzman, A. (1969) *The Iron Cage: an Historical Interpretation of Max Weber*. New York: Grossett & Dunlap.

Mommsen, W. and De Moor, J. (eds) (1992) *European Expansion and the Law*. Oxford: Berg.

Nakamura, K. (1962) *The Formation of Modern Japan: As Viewed from Legal History*. Tokyo: The Centre for East Asian Cultural Studies.

Newby, H. (1977) Reflections on the Study of Suffolk farmworkers, in Bell and Newby (1977).

Outhwaite, W. and Ray, L. (2005) *Social Theory and Postcommunism*. Oxford: Blackwell.

Parsons, T. (1937) *The Structure of Social Action*. New York: McGraw Hill.

Parsons, T. (1951) *The Social System*. London: Routledge.

Parsons, T. and Shils, E. (1951) *Toward a General Theory of Action*. New York: Harper Row.

Pearce, F. (1989) *The Radical Durkheim*. London: Unwin Hyman.

Pearce, F. (2005) Foucault and the 'Hydra-Headed Monster': the College de Sociologie and the two Acephales, in Beaulieu, A. and Gabbard, D. (eds) (2005) *Michel Foucault and Power Today*, Lanham: Lexington Books.

Pearce, F. (2003) The College de Sociologie and French Social Thought, *Economy and Society*. 20(1): 1.

Pearce, F. and Woodiwiss, A. (2001) Reading Foucault as a realist, in Lopez and Potter (2001).

Platt, J. (1996) *A History of Sociological Research Methods in America*. New York: Cambridge University Press.

Popper, K. (1963) *Conjectures and Refutations: The Growth of Scientific Knowledge*. London: Routledge.

Potter, J. and Wetherell, M. (1989) *Discourse and Social Psychology*. London: Sage.

Powers, C. (2004) *Making Sense of Social Theory: A Practical Introduction*. Lanham: Rowan & Littlefield.

Prado, C. (1995) *Starting with Foucault: An Introduction to Genealogy*. Boulder: Westview Press.

Ragin, C. (1994) *Constructing Social Research*. Thousand Oaks: Pine Forge Press.

Resnick, S. and Wolfe, R. (1987) *Knowledge and Class: A Marxian Critique of Political Economy*. Chicago: University of Chicago Press.

Riesman, D. (1950) *The Lonely Crowd*. New Haven: Yale University Press.

Riesman, D. and Watson, J. (1964) The Sociability Project: a chronicle of frustration and achievement, in Hammond (1964).

Robertson, R. (1990) Mapping the global condition: globalization as the central concept, in Featherstone (1990).

Robertson, R. and Turner, B. (eds) (1991) *Talcott Parsons: Theorist of Modernity*. London: Sage.

Rose, N. (1999) *Power of Freedom*. Cambridge: Cambridge University Press.

Ruccio, D., Resnick, S. and Wolff, R. (1991) Class beyond the nation state, *Capital and Class*. 43: 25–41.

Rustin, M. (2004) Private solutions to public problems. Mimeo, Department of Cultural Studies, University of East London.

Sandage, S. (2005) *Born Losers: a History of Failure in America*. Cambridge: Harvard University Press.

Saussure, F. de (1974) *Course in General Linguistics*. London: Fontana.

Savage, M. (2000) *Class Analysis and Social Transformation*. Oxford: Oxford University Press.

Seale, C. (ed.) (1998) *Researching Society and Culture*. London: Sage.

Seizlet, E. (1992) European Law and Tradition in Japan during the Meiji Era, 1868–1912, in Mommsen and de Moor (1992).

Sennett, R. (1977) *The Fall of Public Man*. New York: Norton.

Seuren, P. (1998) *Western Linguistics: an Historical Introduction*. Oxford: Blackwell.

Shieh, G. (1992) *Boss Island*. New York: Peter Lang.

Shoemaker, P., Tankard, J. and Lasorsa, D. (2004) *How to Build Social Science Theories*. Thousand Oaks: Sage.

Smith, T.C. (1959) *The Agrarian Origins of Modern Japan*. Stanford: Stanford University Press.

Sutton, P. (1994) Metropolitan Artisans and the Discourse of the Trade: 1750–1825, unpublished PhD Dissertation, Department of Sociology, University of Essex.

Stedman-Jones, S. (2001) *Durkheim Reconsidered*. Cambridge: Polity.

Stinchcombe, A. (1968) *Constructing Social Theories*. Chicago: University of Chicago Press.

Thornton, D. (1998) *The Scholar in his Study: Ownership and Experience in Renaissance Italy*. New Haven: Yale University Press.

Tolman, E. (1951) A psychological model, in Parsons and Shils (1951).

Tomlinson, J. (1999) *Globalisation and Culture*. Cambridge: Polity.

Tong, R. (1998) *Feminist Thought: a more comprehensive introduction*. Boulder: Westview Press.

Tonkiss, F. (1998) Using text and speech: content and discourse analysis, in Seale (1998).

Traugott, M. (1978) *Emile Durkheim on Institutional Analysis*. Chicago: University of Chicago Press.

Trigg, R. (1981) *Reality at Risk*. Brighton: Harvester.

Trombadori, D. (1991) *Foucault: Remarks on Marx*. New York: Semiotext.

Turner, B. and Hamilton, P. (eds) *Citizenship: Critical Concepts*. London: Routledge.

Turner, J. (1994) The failure of sociology to institutionalize cumulative theorizing, in Hage (2002).

Van der Piji, K. (1997) *The Making of an Atlantic Ruling Class*. New York: Norton.

Wallerstein, I. (2004) *World Systems Analysis: an introduction*. Charlotte: Duke University Press.

Weber, M. (1930) *The Protestant Ethic and the Spirit of Capitalism*. London: Unwin University Press.

Weber, M. (1947) *The Theory of Social and Economic Organisation (excerpts from Economy and Society)*. Glencoe: The Free Press.

Weber, M. (1949) *The Methodology of the Social Sciences*. New York: The Free Press.

Weber, M. (1968) *Economy and Society*, 2 vols. Berkeley: University of California Press.

Whitely, R. (1992) *Business Systems in East Asia*. London: Sage.

Whyte, W.F. (1963) *The Organization Man*. Harmondsworth: Penguin.

Winch, P. (1958) *The Idea of a Social Science*. London: Routledge.

Wittfogel, K. (1957) *Oriental Despotism*. Oxford: Oxford University Press.

Wittgenstein, L. (1922) *Tractatus Logicus Philosophicus*. Republished in 2001. London: Routledge.

Wittgenstein, L. (1963) *Philosophical Investigations*. Oxford: Blackwell.

Wolfe, A. (1988) The Cultural Sources of the Reagan Revolution: the anti-modern legacy, in Kymlicka and Matthews (1988).

Woodiwiss, A. (1990a) *Social Theory After Postmodernism: Rethinking Production, Law and Class*. London: Pluto.

Woodiwiss, A. (1990b) *Rights v. Conspiracy: a Sociological Essay on the History of Labour Law in the United States*. Oxford: Berg.

Woodiwiss, A. (1990c) Rereading Japan: capitalism, possession and the necessity of hegemony, in Abercrombie *et al.* (1990).

Woodiwiss, A. (1992) *Law, Labour and Society in Japan*. London: Routledge.

Woodiwiss, A. (1993) *Postmodernity USA: The Crisis of Social Modernism in the Postwar United States*. London: Sage.

Woodiwiss, A. (1998) *Globalisation, Human Rights and Labour Law in Pacific Asia*. Cambridge: Cambridge University Press.

Woodiwiss, A. (2001) *The Visual in Social Theory*. London: Athlone.

Woodiwiss, A. (2003) *Making Human Rights Work Globally*. London: Glasshouse.

Wright, E.O. (1985) *Classes*. London: Verso.

Wright, E.O. and Singelmann, J. (1982) Proletarianization in the changing American class structure, *American Journal of Sociology*, 88 (supp.): 176.

Yates, F. (1979) *The Occult Philosophy in the Elizabethan Age*. London: Routledge & Kegan Paul.

Index